Airlines For the Rest Of Us
The Rise and Fall of America's Local Service Airlines

Stan Solomon

Contributing Editor, Airways magazine

iUniverse, Inc.
New York   Bloomington

Airlines for the Rest of Us

The Rise and Fall of America's Local Service Airlines

Copyright © 2008 by Stanley Solomon

All rights reserved. No part of this book may be used or reproduced by any means, graphic, electronic, or mechanical, including photocopying, recording, taping or by any information storage retrieval system without the written permission of the publisher except in the case of brief quotations embodied in critical articles and reviews.

The views expressed in this work are solely those of the author and do not necessarily reflect the views of the publisher, and the publisher hereby disclaims any responsibility for them.

iUniverse books may be ordered through booksellers or by contacting:

iUniverse
1663 Liberty Drive
Bloomington, IN 47403
www.iuniverse.com
1-800-Authors (1-800-288-4677)

Because of the dynamic nature of the Internet, any Web addresses or links contained in this book may have changed since publication and may no longer be valid. The views expressed in this work are solely those of the author and do not necessarily reflect the views of the publisher, and the publisher hereby disclaims any responsibility for them.

ISBN: 978-0-595-48443-0 (pbk)
ISBN: 978-0-595-60538-5 (ebk)

Printed in the United States of America

iUniverse rev. date: 10/20/08

Acknowledgements

Thanks to Mr. John Wegg, Editor/Publisher of *Airways* magazine, for providing the photographs used in this book, for providing much useful material during the initial research phase, and for his general support and encouragement,

Thanks to Mr. R.E.G. (Ron) Davies, Curator for Air Transport at the National Air & Space Museum (NASM), for providing access to the truly remarkable trove of airline information which he has accumulated.

Thanks to the many librarians who helped during the research phase – specifically the staff at NASM's Archives and Library, at the library maintained by the Air Transport Association, and at the New York Public Library's Science, Industry, and Business Research Library well as its Mid-Manhattan branch library.

Apologies to anyone else who helped but whom I've neglected to mention. Attribute it to an aging memory.

And, finally, thanks to my wife, Gwen, for her constant encouragement and for putting up with my mood swings during the creation of this book.

Stan Solomon
New York, NY
June, 2008

Contents

Acknowledgements v

Introduction ix

Chapter 1: Route Planning 1

Chapter 2: Preflight 6

Chapter 3: A Long Slow Climb 28

Chapter 4: A Change of Planes 34

Chapter 5: Jet-Propelled 44

Chapter 6: Window Seat 54

Chapter 7: In-Flight Entertainment 72

Chapter 8: Business Class 90

Chapter 9: A Slight Course Deviation 100

Chapter 10: Off the Radar Scope 106

Chapter 11: Ground Stopped 123

Bibliography 134

Appendix 1 : Museum Pieces 138

Appendix 2: Locals On the Web 144

Index 149

Introduction

If you're reading this, chances are you're an aviation buff. And probably one of those fascinated by (obsessed with?) commercial aviation. You know the telltale signs. Drive past the airport and you find yourself slowing, hoping to catch a glimpse of some, any, airliner on very short final, or one just lifting off. You stand transfixed watching a silver dot leave a white contrail against the daytime sky, or the rhythmic pulse of red anti-collision lights tracing a path against the inky night sky. In the terminal you are transfixed by the view out the window – even if it's dark out. You eagerly volunteer to drive people to or from the airport – and you make sure to bring along your airband scanner. At the airport you'll pass a uniformed crew-member and smile, hoping that he or she will recognize you as part of the secret fraternity.

But sometimes we commercial aviation buffs, so caught up by this incredibly complex industry, forget the real purpose of it all. We forget that this multi-billion-dollar industry is really about connecting places – big cities with other big cities, or with smaller or mid-size communities, and even smaller communities with their counterparts. We forget that it's about giving people, be they once-a-year leisure travelers or once-a-week business travelers, the ability to get from Peoria to Portland, Maine or Portland, Oregon – to visit Paris, France or even Paris, Texas.

Which was the logic behind the thinking of a government agency in 1944, when it created the opportunity for an entirely new class of airline in this country. That agency, the Civil Aeronautics Board (C. A.B.) believed, or had been persuaded, that not all places in this country had an equivalent level of regularly scheduled airline service. Although the major and mid-sized cities were adequately served, other places were not – and the major airlines, with large portions of their fleets dedicated to the war effort, didn't seem as if they were too interested in ever remedying this inequity.

So the C.A.B. tried an experiment – it would create an opportunity for entrepreneurs "fit, willing, and able" to meet specific standards to obtain temporary-but-renewable certificates. They would provide airline service to those places that had none. These airlines would be called "Feeders," for their main purpose would be to pick up passengers at intermediate points and convey them to a terminus, where, theoretically, they would be 'fed' to one of the major carriers to continue their travels.

So how is this different from the role played today by the various airlines' regional partners, such as American Eagle, Continental Express, Delta Connection, etc.? The answer: vastly different! Today's regionals have no identity of their own; instead they are 'branded' with the colors of the larger airlines that they service, so as to create the illusion of seamless connectivity. Also the financial arrangements are much more complex, and in some cases, such as that which exists between Comair and Delta, the regional actually is a wholly-owned subsidiary of the larger entity.

The Feeders/Locals, were a different breed – each with its own colors and identity and fiercely independent, definitely not associated with any one major airline. If anything, they were associated with their geographic region, and that became each one's unique identity. Mohawk, in the Northeast, capitalized on that area's Native American heritage (in ways that today could never pass the test of political correctness) while Southern reveled in the heritage of The Old South. The Feeders/Locals were startups struggling to establish themselves, and one way to stand out was to gjve their airplanes dramatic names, like *Pacemaker* and *PamperJet*. Startups today, like jetBlue, still name their airplanes, but when's the last time anyone saw a quirky name on a United Express or Continental Connection airplane? The regional affiliates are expected to be good corporate soldiers, with no individuality. Thus, even though they may be operated by totally different companies, an American Eagle RJ (Regional Jet) serving, say, Portland, Maine looks exactly like its counterpart serving Portland, Oregon.

But colorful identities are not the only difference. The Feeders/Locals offered a much higher level of service to their communities, and that service was maintained at a level acceptable to the very watchful eye of the C.A.B. For example, consider Bradford, a town of 9,000 in northwest Pennsylvania that is home to the Zippo Lighter company. In the era of the Local Service Airlines Bradford was served by Allegheny (progenitor of today's US Airways), which offered service to Washington, D.C., to New York City, and to other places in Pennsylvania. Today residents of Bradford have far fewer options. Thanks to the federally- subsidized Essential Air Service (see Chapter 11, "Ground Stopped") Bradford still has three arrivals and three departures per weekday, dropping to two each on weekends. Yet it is impossible to fly to any place other than Dulles International Airport, 223 miles away in the Virginia suburbs outside Washington, D.C. via United Express. Which means that anyone whose destination is Our Nation's Capital must endure a 30-mile bus or taxi ride to downtown, and anyone whose destination is elsewhere must endure the notorious confusion of Dulles International when changing airplanes. Also, the cost is prohibitive, at $576 for a roundtrip from Bradford to Washington. And the final insult? After decades of continuous service, Bradford was abandoned recently by US Airways, scion of Allegheny, when it ordered its US Airways Express partner to drop that city from its list of places served.

For small cities life was different under the locals. They offered a reliable mode of transit in their particular region, providing a link between smaller communities and the larger cities. True, flying was not yet a form of mass transit and so there were not that many leisure travelers, but the business community appreciated the service offered by these airlines. A salesperson could fly, rather than drive, around his territory or an executive from a smallish town, say Colorado Springs, could attend a regional meeting in Salt Lake City and be home the same day. That service was the reason behind the C.A.B.'s decision to create this new level of airline, and why they became known as Local *Service* Carriers.

For most people it is difficult to imagine the service lost when the Locals disappeared. But with a little effort it may be demonstrated. The author selected five one-way trips typical for 1955, the Local's early DC-3 period, and converted the fares (published in that year's *Official Airline Guide) from 1955 to 2008 dollars (this was done in June, 2008) to show what each trip would cost today. The results came from a very easy-to-use calculator featured on the Federal Reserve Bank of Minneapolis web site. First, a basic fact: what cost one dollar ($1.00) in 1955 would cost eight times as much ($8.04) in 2008. Or the reverse: something in 2008 that costs one dollar (if anything) would have set you back just twelve cents (0.12) in 1955.*

Then came inspiration – rather than simply converting the fares, why not use a travel web site to see which of these trips were still possible and, if so, what each would cost in June, 2008. The Expedia.com site was selected for its ease of use. For each trip the author requested a one-way trip on a far-off mid-week day, January 20, 2009, to avoid any potential price penalty for holidays and to get the lowest possible fares. As this book went to press, these were the (sometimes surprising) results, arranged from low to high in 1955 fares:

Trip 1: Walla Walla, Washington to Seattle, Washington aboard West Coast. In 1955 the one-way trip would have cost $14.00 ($112.63 in 2008 dollars). According to Expedia.com, in June, 2008 there were three departures available, actually for a lower price of $104.50. So score one for Alaska Airlines!

Trip 2: Athens, Georgia to Tuscaloosa, Alabama aboard Southern. The 1955 one-way fare was $17.84 ($143.52 in 2008 dollars). But don't reach for your credit card – according to Expedia.com, it was IMPOSSIBLE to fly commercially into Tuscaloosa. The airport received no scheduled service, either from Athens or even from Atlanta. For more on situations such as this, be sure to read Chapter 11, "Ground Stopped."

Trip 3: Green Bay, Wisconsin to Detroit, Michigan aboard North Central. 1955's one-way fare was $21.60 ($173.77 in 2008 money). According to Expedia.com, the trip was available…lowest price $244.00 – but the potential traveler had to be prepared for a journey of 8.5 hours, with two changes of aircraft! There was a one-hour non-stop available, but its cost was an incredible $507.00. That would be $63.02 in 1955 dollars…basically triple what it cost back then.

Trip 4: Prescott, Arizona to Los Angeles, California with Bonanza. 1955's fare was $23.75 ($191.06 in 2008 dollars). Now here's a bargain! Again thanks to Alaska Airlines, the 2008 price was just $101. Of course, there's only one daily departure, an early-morning 07:45 flight. And, based on reports that, as of October 2008 Alaska, like many other carriers (see Chapter 11, "Ground Stopped") would implement severe cutbacks in flying because of surging fuel costs, there is always the possibility that little Prescott would be one of the cities dropped.

Trip 5: Myrtle Beach, South Carolina to Louisville, Kentucky on Piedmont. It was $36.55 in 1955 ($294.04 in 2008 value). Delta's $417 price seemed a tad high – especially when one factored in that this eight hour trip meant changing planes both in Atlanta and in Orlando, Florida. It was possible to do the trip in 3.5 hours and change planes only once – but for an astronomical $631 dollars (that's $78.44 in 1955 dollars, or double Piedmont's 1955 fare).

Of course there are many, many reasons for this change of fortune, and it is not the place of this book to discuss or debate the current condition of the airline industry in this super-competitive, post 9/11, ridiculously-high fuel cost world. In fact, as this book was being prepared for press, the evening news was full of stories that, because of fuel prices, not only were the major airlines being forced to curtail capacity, but that such cuts were bound to affect service to the smaller communities, which were already seeing cutbacks. Although this new problem is discussed in Chapter 11, "Ground Stopped," it is not the purpose of this book to attempt to keep up with constantly changing current conditions.

Rather its purpose is to tell the story and honor the memory of a group of airlines little-remembered today, and to recall an era when a government agency both regulated and protected the airline industry, attempting to maintain the economic well-being of that industry while serving the average citizen – whether he or she lived in a major city or a small town.

So, as 'our heroes' up on the flight deck often say, relax and enjoy the trip.

Chapter 1: Route Planning

First, a little background information, to put things into perspective. The story of the Local Service Airlines begins in a very different era – different because not only were the airlines tightly regulated by a government agency but because these 'regula<u>tees</u>,' to coin a phrase, actually welcomed the control and oversight of their regula<u>tor</u>, the Civil Aeronautics Board, or C.A.B.

Why so? Because with such regulation the airlines were finally able to turn a profit. Why so? Because <u>before</u> such regulation the airline industry was in chaos – economic chaos. For a thorough understanding it is necessary to read parts of R.E.G. Davies' authoritative *Airlines of the United States Since 1914*, Henry Ladd Smith's *Airways: The History of Commercial Aviation in the United States*, Robert van der Linden's *Airlines & Air Mail*, Nick A. Komons' *Bonfires to Beacons*, or any other respected history of U.S. commercial aviation. But here's the condensed version.

By the mid-1930s, new airlines were constantly springing up, vying with each other by under-bidding for the more lucrative mail routes offered by the U.S. Post Office (as it was then called) and competing to attract the relatively limited number of people sufficiently 'brave' to want to travel by air. Between 1934 and 1936 there were 19 domestic airlines, of which only six could show a profit, an anemic $134,000, while combined losses reached $3.5 million. Matters became so bad that the Air Transport Association begged the government for help.

Relief finally came via the landmark Civil Aeronautics Act of 1938. Signed by President Roosevelt on June 23 of that year, it created the Civil Aeronautics Authority (which became the C.A.B. in 1940) and thus established a 40-year pattern of comprehensive and coordinated government control of aviation. Any airline, whether or not it planned to carry mail, now needed a Certificate of Public Convenience and Necessity. Those certificates, to which pre-1938 airlines had Grandfather Rights, became a "check against unnecessary competition," as Smith writes, by preventing any carrier from either starting or abandoning a route without approval. The airlines also needed approval for just about everything they did, except arrange schedules and choose equipment. Ticket prices and tariffs for carrying packages required formal approval, and so the self-destructive fare-wars became just a bad memory. Or, as Davies writes, the 1938 legislation "stabilized the administration of the airlines on a rational basis."

Now, under C.A.B. rules, airlines could compete, but on service rather than on fares, which were subject to C.A.B. approval. Airlines received an indirect subsidy in the form of compensation for carrying the U.S. mail. One airline could not acquire another unless the tobe-acquired was in severe financial difficulty, and there had to be safeguards for both employees and places served. Routes were awarded only after lengthy hearings involving testimony by residents of the area and by carriers already serving the route.

The changes worked. With C.A.B. oversight keeping a lid on competition, and with the arrival of "modern" all-metal airliners such as Boeing's 247D and Douglas Aircraft's DC-2 (which would morph into the famed DC-3), the airlines were becoming profitable. In the pre-Pearl Harbor months of 1941, the domestic airlines would carry four million passengers, or four-and-one-half times as many as they had in all of 1935. But everything was about to change.

As of December 7, 1941 the U.S. was at war on two fronts, and the airlines would soon be sending many of their airplanes to join the war effort. Under an agreement brokered with President Roosevelt by the Air Transport Association's president, Edgar S. Gorrell, the airlines had voluntarily relinquished just over half of their fleet to the U.S. Ferrying Command (later the Air Transport Command) to move materiel and equipment. Compounding matters was the fact that any uniformed serviceman had automatic priority in securing an increasingly scarce airline seat.

So capacity was down and seats were scarce. And in many places there were no seats at all, because no airlines flew there. Those places without scheduled air service began to feel second rate, and some began to ask why they were being left out. Their requests went not to the airlines but to their congressmen and senators, who passed them along to the C.A.B. Or so legend has it. Cynics claim that the letter-writing may have been partially encouraged by the airlines, even then eager for new routes. That may explain why the C.A.B. asked the Air Transport Association to please have its member airlines refrain from encouraging further 'Write-your-Congressman' campaigns.

But there was another force at work – good old American entrepreneurship. At the C.A.B. there was a backlog of applications from businessmen eager to start airline service. One of these was West Coast Airlines' founder Nick Bez who, as early as 1941, had proposed an airline to carry mail and packages to and from the remote Pacific Northwest communities where he, a penniless immigrant, had arrived years earlier and where he had made his fortune serving those fishing communities (see Chapter 2, "Preflight").

So conditions were right for a 'perfect storm' – economically. On the one hand was the C.A.B. and its beliefs that: (1) air travel was such a good thing that its blessings should be extended to as many people as possible; (2) decisions were to be made in an orderly and impartial manner; and (3) airlines, which deserved to earn reasonable profits, should be nurtured and supported. Playing right into this spirit of altruism and fairness was the growing demand for scheduled airline service, both from un-served communities and from potential entrepreneurs.

So, according to a C.A.B. *Annual Report*, on March 22, 1943, that agency moved, ordering "an investigation into the general problems involved in extending air transportation to additional communities and localities in the United States" especially where "…such transportation may not appear warranted under usual economic conditions or under existing standards of operation." Fifteen months later, on July 11, 1944 (one month after D-Day), the C.A.B. announced its findings in Docket No. 857, Investigation of Local, Feeder, and Pick-up

Air Service. The answer was 'Yes,' the C.A.B. was willing to begin certification hearings for an entirely new class of airline – the Feeder or Local Service Airline.

But theirs was a very qualified 'yes,' as a closer analysis of Docket 857 reveals. The C.A.B. constantly collected and analyzed data, and this data suggested that passengers were not about to come racing to the airport, suitcases in hand, just because their town had new airline service. Furthermore, especially east of the Mississippi, where cities were not that far apart, any airline would face instant competition from private automobiles, from railroads, and even from bus lines. Airplanes, the C.A.B. admitted, were more profitable on long-haul trips, and could actually lose money on short-haul trips.

So why do it? Because it had never been done before. The challenge exists, said the C.A.B., and there were applicants eager to meet such challenge. Besides, the public just might benefit beyond present expectations. Thus it would allow the creation of this new class of airline to proceed. But within certain limitations. This would be an experiment. Therefore, the Certificates of Public Convenience and Necessity would be temporary, subject to review after three years, at which time the certificate-holder would be obligated to demonstrate that renewal would not burden the government with unreasonable costs. In fact, the C.A.B. insisted, permanent certification would be allowed only to operators who had made a conscientious effort to reduce costs to the government.

But why not give us these new routes, complained the existing airlines, for we can certainly contain costs? As George Eads, foremost of the Locals' critics, explains in *The Local Service Airline Experiment*, the C.A.B. held hearings on the question, and during those year-long hearings the established airlines offered many reasons why they should be given the routes, including: (1) It would be less costly for an existing airline to add destinations than for a start-up to begin from scratch; (2) Any losses incurred from short-haul operations could be absorbed by profits generated in regular operations, something a new carrier with no existing profitable routes could never hope to do; and (3) They already had the expertise born of experience and they had the all-weather equipment that would guarantee better service than the Locals projected.

This may all be true, said the C.A.B. in its "Opinion," but nevertheless the routes will be operated only by brand-new airlines. Low traffic potential on these new routes required taking advantage of every possible economy, and this could be done only by new carriers whose applications indicated that they understood how to offer "less luxurious standards of service." They fully expected that these startups would make use of smaller and more economical aircraft, such as the nine-seat Lockheed Electras with which Wisconsin Central (later North Central) would begin service.

But some suggest that the CAB was actually suspicious of the existing airlines' motives, believing that they were simply seeking to eliminate possible future competitors or to capture passengers exclusively for their mainline operations, as today's big airlines do in their code-sharing arrangements with regionals. More cynical still is the theory that the CAB did not want to jeopardize the health of the recovering airlines. If operating these new Feeder routes might prove disastrously unprofitable, better that a startup take the blow rather than an existing airline. As a Flight magazine editorial said almost forty years later, "The local carriers contributed measurably to the growth and rapid development of the trunk lines by relieving them from unprofitable short haul traffic."

Whatever its reasons, in 1944 the CAB made a fateful decision. It became the midwife for the birth of an entirely new class of airline, and that decision changed the face of commercial aviation in the U.S.

So that's how the Local Service Carriers came to be. In the following chapters we will explore, briefly, the startup history of each, trace their growth from quirky, even fumbling, fledglings to names that even today, almost 60 years later, are still recognizable as players, like Piedmont and Frontier. And, if you've ever flown on US Airways, you are traveling with a direct descendant of Allegheny, one of the original Locals.

So come on along as we trace the history of these airlines.

Chapter 2: Preflight

Almost four months after its announcement that it would entertain the idea of a new type of airline, the C.A.B. was besieged by applications – some 700 of them. Some were innovative – offering to use the relatively new helicopter; while others were downright flaky – such as the two that proposed using lighter-than-air craft. But the rest were serious and straight-forward, and it was now the C.A.B.'s task to find those with the most merit.

That task took quite a while – almost two years, which would not surprise later critics of that federal agency. To give it its due, however, it must be noted that it was the agency's goal to ensure fairness and democracy. Thus it followed a rigorous and stringent procedure. After sorting applications by geographic region, it would set teams of examiners to investigate the applicant's relative merits and to hear testimony by all interested parties. The examiners then presented their recommendations to the five Board members, who would have the final say before any routes could be awarded. The C.A.B. called such a process a "Case," and it was already handling other cases dealing with the existing airlines. Thus it was not until March of 1946 that it was ready to announce the results of the Rocky Mountain Air Service Case, the very first dealing with local service routes.

It would take several more years to handle all the Cases, but eventually some 26 local service carriers received their temporary certificates. Of that number, only 13 survived past 1955. The purpose of this "Preflight" chapter is to tell, by order of first passenger service, how each local service airline came to be, from Pioneer – the first to fly and the first to disappear – through Air New England, the youngest local service airline (service began in 1970). Finally, after these startup tales, there are brief summaries of the 'also-rans' –locals that never quite made it.

Q: So…which <u>was</u> the very first local service airline?

A: There are many "firsts," *i.e.* first to incorporate, first to operate as an un-certificated intrastate carrier, first to receive a formal C.A.B. Certificate, and first to actually start certificated passenger service. Then, for boasting rights, some Locals pointed further back, to their predecessors' actual start of certificated passenger service, as Frontier did when, although it did not operate as Frontier until July of 1950, it claimed the November, 1946 date of its major predecessor, Monarch Airways. **Thus the order below, reflecting such practice, includes the date of first certificated passenger service of the airline <u>or</u> of its predecessor:**

1. Pioneer (Essair) - August 25, 1945 :

True to its name, it <u>was</u> a pioneer – the first feeder to start actual passenger service and, unfortunately, the first well-functioning member of its group to be absorbed by another airline.

Actually its original name wasn't Pioneer but Essair – meaning '<u>E</u>fficiency, <u>s</u>afety, and <u>s</u>peed in the <u>air</u>.' But in its original incarnation it never spent very much time in the air. In January 1939, when the

C.A.B. was still the C.A.A., and long before anyone began thinking about Feeder airlines, this carrier had been incorporated as an officially sanctioned experiment. Founded by Major William "Bill" Long, a former World War I pilot and ex-barnstormer who was a Fixed Base Operator (FBO) at Dallas' Love Field, it was supposed to fly between Houston and Amarillo by way of Abilene. But it survived only six months, and some question if it ever carried any passengers. It had been blasted out of the air by Braniff, which formally protested this invasion of its "sphere of influence" guaranteed by the Grandfather Rights of its certificate.

This started a lawyer-duel, and, after much wrangling, the C.A.B. said that, yes, Essair was better qualified to operate that Houston –

Amarillo route than any trunk airline. Because its schedule was more receptive to people's needs. Their decision came down on November 5, 1943, eight months <u>before</u> Docket 857, establishing feeders as a new class of airline (see Chapter 1, "Route Planning"). Essair received a Certificate of Public Convenience and Necessity allowing it to transport persons, property and mail between the terminal point Houston and the intermediate points Austin, San Angelo, Abilene, and Lubbock, and the terminal point Amarillo."

Actual passenger service would not start until August 25, 1945, using three 12-seat Lockheed 10-A Electras, a larger version of the type airplane in which Amelia Earhart had disappeared eight years earlier. But the little twin-tailed twin-engine ships proved inadequate for many reasons, including their lack of instrument flight capability, and so by spring 1946 Essair had purchased four Douglas C-47s for $20 thousand each and had them converted to 24-seat DC-3s. They went into service exactly a year after the start-up date, and the company boasted that for the first time a feeder line was operating with equipment identical to that of some of the trunk carriers.

In spring 1946 the directors, noting that no one associated " Essair Lines" with air travel, officially dropped that name in favor of " Pioneer Air Lines," and several months later, on November 27, 1946, the C.A.B. announced the results of Texas-Oklahoma Route Case, which effectively doubled Pioneer's mileage. In a few years it would cover much of Texas and reach west as far as Albuquerque in New Mexico.

2. Frontier - November 27, 1946 :

This legendary airline – with its spotless safety record and a well-deserved reputation for serving the American West for four decades, actually began its existence as a merger of three local service carriers: Arizona, Challenger, and Monarch.

A). Arizona – It was the weakest of the three components that would merge to become Frontier. Phoenix-based, Arizona Airways had begun as an intrastate scenic operator in March 1946. But despite the backing of the powerful department-store Goldwater family, which also produced U.S. senator and presidential candidate Barry Goldwater, it never achieved financial stability. In 1948 it received an Arizona – Texas route award, but never managed to start actual service.

B). Challenger – The Rocky Mountain States Area Case authorized a startup calling itself Summit Airways to operate routes between Montana, Colorado, and Utah. On February 2, 1947 Summit renamed itself Challenger Airlines, and with two ex-Capital Airlines DC-3s it began servicing its first route on May 3, 1947 – Salt Lake City to Denver with stops in Kemmerer, Rock Springs, Rawlings, Laramie, Cheyenne. It would eventually link ten Wyoming communities to Denver, Billings, and Salt Lake City

C). Monarch – Although last alphabetically, it was the sturdy stock onto which the other two would be grafted. Denver-based, it was founded by Ray M. Wilson with financial support from the business manager of the *Denver Post*. In March 1946, still calling itself Ray Wilson, Inc., it won certification in the C.A.B.'s Rocky Mountain States Area Case to operate Feeder service between Denver, Salt Lake City, Albuquerque – and a host of intermediate points. By its start date of November 27, 1946 it operated two DC-3s and was calling itself " Monarch Air Lines: The Scenic Skyway of the West."

Since both Monarch and Challenger each served Denver and Salt Lake City, the idea of merger began to make sense. First came a shared Denver maintenance base and sales department. Then the C.A.B. agreed that in such a sparsely populated area one strong airline serving seven states from north to south was better than three struggling airlines. In December 1949 Monarch was allowed to buy Challenger and five months later, in April 1950, it acquired the ailing Arizona. Two months later, with a fleet of 12 DC-3 'Sunliners,' the newly named Frontier set out to begin building a reputation for on-time performance and service excellence that would endure till 1986.

3. Pacific (' Southwest') – December 2, 1946 :

Fittingly, in the days when California still meant Hollywood and Silicon Valley was unheard of, the local most associated with that state was bankrolled by a group of the Hollywood elite. Producer Leland Hayward (*Mister Roberts*, *The Spirit of St. Louis*, etc.) had been a WWI pilot and also served on Transcontinental and Western's board of directors. He persuaded a slew of box-office names, including Jimmy Stewart, Henry Fonda, and Ginger Rogers, to invest in this venture.

With the war about to end, Hayward and his partners in a paper airline calling itself Southwest (no relation to the current low-fare carrier) joined the other applicants seeking certificates. The C.A.B.'s West Coast Case (May 1946) awarded it routes from Los Angeles to San Francisco and from San Francisco to Medford, Oregon (which was the southern terminus of West Coast's routes). Southwest's first airline service began in December that year. Its routes served towns less than 50 miles apart, which meant stage lengths of 25 minutes. Competing against auto traffic, Southwest also advertised quick turnarounds, which it called "two-minute stops." Except when refueling, one engine was kept running while the "purser" handed deplaning passengers their luggage and welcomed boarding passengers. Then, like the gripman on a San Francisco cable car, he rang a bell to notify the pilots that all was ready for yet another departure.

Southwest enjoyed a weird "give-and-take" relationship with the C.A.B. In December, 1949 that agency gave the airline the Los Angeles – Phoenix route – and then took it back four months later, giving it to Bonanza in 1952. But when Southwest acquired Martin 2-0-2s it received better treatment than Pioneer, its counterpart in Texas. The agency allowed Southwest to keep the airplanes, arguing that it was simply adding to – not replacing – its entire fleet.

On March 6, 1958, Southwest formally became Pacific Air Lines. Turboprop Fairchild F-27s would soon join the fleet, and by 1966 it would be operating Boeing 727s.

4. West Coast - December 3, 1946 :

Anyone who doubts that the U.S. represents unbelievable opportunity is hereby referred to the story of one Nicholas ("Nick") Bez, an immigrant who arrived here almost penniless and who went on to start several successful fish-packing companies, start an airline later absorbed by Pan American, and found West Coast Airways.

Born on August 25, 1895, in Yugo Slavia, (stet.), the 15-year-old Bez emigrated to the United States in September, 1910, and eventually made his way to Tacoma, Washington, where he worked various manual jobs before moving on to Ketchikan in Southeast Alaska to become a fisherman. By 1917 he had his own fishing boat, by 1919 he had acquired two more, and in 1927 he had started the "Peril Straits Packing Company," which had $200,000 annual revenue. The absence of any roads in this part of Alaska provided an opportunity. In 1931 the entrepreneurial Bez started the Alaska Southern Airways, a charter operator whose fleet would grow to include three Lockheed Vega 5-Bs, a Fairchild, and a Loening Commuter. In 1933 the little "airline" began offering fairly regular Juneau – Ketchikan – Seattle trips. But the Pan American subsidiary Pacific Alaska Airways wanted no competition on its Alaska – Seattle routes and so, on November 13, 1934 it bought Bez's Alaska Southern.

But Bez was not through with the airline business, although he now shifted his attention to "The Lower 48." He realized that an airline transferring packages and express from small West Coast communities to the trunk airlines would probably make money. So, on June 7, 1941, he applied to the C.A.B. for a Certificate of Public Convenience and Necessity for his proposed airline, to be called West Coast Airlines, Inc. But war was on the horizon and all applications were on hold. Finally, the C.A.B.'s 1944 Docket 857 started the ball rolling, and on May 22, 1946 the C.A.B.'s West Coast Case gave Bez permission to operate an airline carrying mail, freight, and express.

Passenger service began on December 5, 1946, with West Coast serving the two primary cities of The Evergreen Empire – Washington State's Seattle and Oregon's Portland plus the many smaller cities in between. In July 1947 its route was extended south to Medford, close to the Oregon – California border, where passengers would transfer to another local, Southwest Airways (see above). Another transfer point between locals developed in 1950, when West Coast's routes expanded into eastern Washington State, including the city of Spokane, where passengers could connect with Empire Air Lines (see below). Bez realized that Empire's routes represented a wonderful asset, and he petitioned the C.A.B. for permission to acquire that local, which the C.A.B. granted in June 1952. For a few months after the August 1952 completion of the merger the company's timetables were labeled "West Coast Empire Airlines," but soon the " Empire" name disappeared. Bez's white-and-green West Coast 'ScenicLiners' soon became a fixture throughout the Pacific Northwest, which the airline began calling 'Paul Bunyan's Empire.'

5. Texas International (Trans-Texas) – October 11, 1947 :

It has been called The Mouse That Roared. This once quaint little carrier whose "TTA" initials prompted some to dub it either "Tree-Top Airways" or "Tinker-Toy Airways," would later expand its route map across the country and into Mexico and serve as the base for acquisition raids against long-established airlines twice its size. But most of that wild ride came late in its history, after the 1971 rise to power of Frank Lorenzo – aviation entrepreneur extraordinaire. Its early years were a lot calmer.

Its parent was a corporation calling itself Aviation Enterprises, Inc., incorporated under the laws of Texas on November 14, 1944. The person filing the papers of incorporation was R. Earl McKaughan, who for the previous four years had been running Aviation Enterprises, Ltd, an aircraft sales and service company out of Houston Hobby Airport. In 1943 the enterprising McKaughan reasoned that forming a legal corporation would make his application to start an airline more appealing to the C.A.B.

That the C.A.B. was impressed is not clear, but two years later its decision in the Texas-Oklahoma Route Investigation awarded McKaughan's company routes in southern Texas, effective May 12, 1947. A month later McKaughan re-named the company Trans-Texas Airlines and some four months afterwards, on October 11, the airline began service. Its first routes – Houston in the southern part of the state, Dallas to the north, and both San Angelo and San Antonio to the west formed a backwards-facing "C." By 1949 El Paso was the western-most point and Brownsville the southern-most, but it was still serving only Texas. It wouldn't be until April 1953 that TTA's DC-3 'Starliners' would show their Lone Star tails in Arkansas, Louisiana, and Tennessee.[1]

By 1969 TTA had already converted its 25 Convair 240 'Silver Liners' to Rolls-Royce Dart-powered Convair 600 'Silver Clouds', was operating seven Douglas DC-9-10 'Pamper Jets', and served Monterrey, Tampico, and Veracruz, Mexico. Then, on April 1, 1969, the new owners changed its name to Texas International. Lorenzo's debut was two years off.

6. Piedmont – February 20, 1948 :

Had fate not intervened it might have been called Camel City Airlines. But Thomas H. (Tom) Davis, changed the name of his "Camel City Flying Service", purchased in 1940 from R.J. Reynolds

Tobacco Company heir Dick Reynolds, to Piedmont Aviation in order to better reflect its geographic region.

"Piedmont," literally "foot of the mountain," refers to the flatlands between the Atlantic Ocean and the mountain ranges of the Appalachians and the Great Smokies. Operating out of Winston-Salem's Smith-Reynold's Airport, Piedmont Aviation became a federally-approved Maintenance, Repair, and Overhaul (MRO) facility as well as one of 14 centers authorized to train World War II pilots. But in January 1944 the War Department pulled the plug on the program. Seeking a new source of revenue, the Board decided that Piedmont Aviation should start an airline. Davis submitted his application in June 1944 and then waited. And waited.

Somehow the company scraped by, having won a government contract to sell surplus airplane parts. Then on April 4, 1947, almost three years later, the C.A.B.'s Southeastern States Case gave Piedmont Aviation a certificate to provide passenger, mail, and freight service on Route 87, between the Ohio River Valley and the Tidewater regions. Faced with the task of creating an airline from scratch, Davis hired several mid-level managers away from Eastern Air Lines and purchased two DC-3s from Colonial Airlines. Service was to start in September, but Charlotte-based State Airlines, which had bid on the same routes, appealed. Then Eastern joined in, claiming that this little start-up had a hidden agenda and was really planning to become a trunk line infringing on its routes.

Even worse, said the Eastern appeal, because only four towns would benefit by getting their first-ever air service, the whole idea was "wasteful, extravagant, and unneeded." Almost a half-year passed until, on December 12, 1947, the C.A.B. ruled in Piedmont's behalf. The Airline Division of Piedmont Aviation was chartered in January 1948 and actual service started on February 20, 1948. That first route linked coastal Wilmington, North Carolina, to the Mid-West's Cincinnati, Ohio, with five intermediate stops – two of which had grass-strip runways.

7. North Central (Wisconsin Central) – February 24, 1948 :

Had a Wisconsin truck manufacturer been able to count on the railroad to get its people to Chicago and Milwaukee, then perhaps North Central would never have been born. But by 1939 passenger train service to little Clintonville, some 35 miles west of Green Bay, was almost non-existent. So the Four Wheel Drive Company (FWDC) traded one of its trucks for a Waco Cabin biplane and began twice-weekly flights to Chicago. Two years later the company added a Howard DGA-15 and increased the frequency of its flights. Now local businessmen were cadging trips, and it soon dawned on management that they were looking at a new way to earn revenue.

In May of 1944 the papers incorporating the little unscheduled shuttle service as Wisconsin Central Airlines were filed. And a few months later FWDC's advertising manager was sent off to Washington, D.C. to see about applying for one of those new "feeder" routes that the C.A.B. had announced. In a letter to a friend he expressed surprise at how complex and time-consuming it was to satisfy all of the C.A.B.'s requirements.

He was in for even bigger surprises. 33 other applicants were seeking to serve the Badger State, and the C.A.B. created the North Central Area Investigation to evaluate their claims. Two years later, in March 1946, a C.A.B. Examiner suggested that, based on its past business practices, perhaps FWDC was seeking to operate this airline not for the public's convenience but for its own. He said the application should be denied. To demonstrate that they were indeed fit, willing, and able to operate an airline in the public interest, FWDC sold the Waco and Howard and purchased two Cessna T-50 Bobcats.

Wisconsin Central would now be an intrastate airline, operating five days each week to Madison, Milwaukee, Wausau, and several other cities. It lasted a half-year, bleeding money until FWDC had to suspend operations in November 1946. The airline idea seemed to be doomed when, on the very last day of 1946, news from Washington changed everything. The C.A.B. had ignored its own Examiner's recommendation and awarded Wisconsin Central 1,400 miles of interstate routes connecting 43 cities, including Chicago, Illinois; Minneapolis, Minnesota; and Duluth, Michigan. But there was a catch – and a big one.

The C.A.B. ruled that there could be absolutely no connection between FWDC and Wisconsin Central. Thus FWDC would have to sell its shares and the airline would have to find new investors. Another 14 months passed before Wisconsin Central finally began service, on February 24, 1948. It had somehow raised enough capital to buy three Lockheed 10-A Electras for $12,000 apiece, paying some $38,000 less than the sticker price of a used DC-3. And led by former TWA executive Hal N. Carr, who at the time was the youngest airline president, the fledgling airline had also relocated to Madison, Wisconsin, the state capital. It acquired its first DC-3s in October 1950. The cost to purchase, overhaul, and acquire spare parts for the six ex- TWA airplanes came to $450,000, or one-quarter of the airline's annual revenue for 1950. But it now had "real" airliners.

Almost two years later, on September 24, 1952, the stockholders approved changing the name to North Central to better reflect the fact that the airline now served a five-state region.

8. Mohawk (Robinson) – September 19, 1948 :

Besides being a professional photographer, C.S. Robinson was also an inventor/businessman – and a licensed pilot. All three skills coalesced to produce an airline entrepreneur.

His inner inventor had developed a temperature-resistant high altitude camera mount which his inner businessman wanted to market. But his home in the central New York state community of Ithaca was several hundred miles from the northern New Jersey manufacturing plant. Driving was tedious and, in that pre-Interstate Highway era, even risky. But his inner pilot came to the rescue. Robinson began flying to New Jersey's Teterboro Airport in his single-engine Fairchild F-24. Then some of his acquaintances began asking to ride along on the relatively swift 80-minute flights.

That's when Robinson's inner-businessman realized that there was a demonstrated demand for air travel and that, since he owned two airplanes, he could meet that demand. Heck, he could start an airline! So on April 1, 1945, four months before the end of World War II, he filed an application with the C.A.B. to operate a feeder airline linking New York's Buffalo, Rochester, Ithaca, Binghamton, and Albany with New York City and far-off Washington, D.C. To demonstrate that he was indeed 'fit, willing, and able' he established the airline division of Robinson Aviation. On August 6 he began an air taxi service between Ithaca and New York City. Because the service flew intrastate, carried no mail, and asked for no subsidy it wasn't subject to C.A.B. control. Passenger demand became so great that he added two Cessna T-50 four-place twins and hired extra pilots, including a former Navy pilot turned law-school student named Robert E. Peach, who would eventually become Mohawk's legendary president. By year's end the Robinson air-taxi service had carried, by various estimates, 900 to 1,200 passengers.

The next year, 1946, brought service to Buffalo (January 22), Binghamton (May 23), and Albany (July 1). And the first "real" airliners – seven-passenger twin-engine Beechcraft D-18s – for the company that on December 1, 1946, began calling itself the Robinson Airline Corporation. Needing cash to expand, Robinson turned to local investors – including Edwin A. Link, inventor of the "Link Trainer," who became a shareholder and who also lent Robinson $75,000 to buy the first of three DC-3s.

Finally, on February 20, 1948 the C.A.B. announced its findings in the Middle Atlantic Air Service Case. Robinson received the right to carry passengers and mail between New York City and a host of upstate communities. Service as a certificated feeder began on September 19, 1948. C.S. Robinson gradually lost interest in running the airline and in June 1949 Peach became general manager. In 1951, celebrating the C.A.B.'s seven-year extension of the original certificate, the company asked employees to help rename their airline. In June 1952 the board of directors chose the name Mohawk over the next two choices: Atlantic and Yankee.

9. Allegheny (All American) – March 7, 1949 :

Today's US Airways, itself an incredible survivor, can trace its existence to a fortuitous mix of some really innovative technology, some clever entrepreneurs, and some government encouragement.

The entrepreneurs were Dr. Lytle Adams and Mr. Richard DuPont, heir to the chemical manufacturing fortune and an aviation enthusiast. DuPont bankrolled Adams's experiments to develop a unique form of air-borne mail delivery and pickup that would be available to every town, whether or not that town had an actual airport. Delivery was simple, for the inbound mail could just be tossed to the ground from the low-flying airplane. Pick-up was accomplished via an ingenious system in which the bag of outbound mail was suspended from a rope strung between two sturdy poles. The pilot would swoop low and snag the mailbag in mid-air, and his assistant would then reel it in and stow it securely.

In 1938, the same year that saw passage of the Civil Aeronautics Act, Adams and DuPont responded to a U.S. Post Office request for bids on an experiment to bring mail service to 54 communities in Pennsylvania, West Virginia, and Ohio. They named their company All American Aviation. The Post Office awarded them a one-year contract, and, after months of preparation, on May 12, 1939, they formally demonstrated their unique system, using single-engine Stinson SR-10C *Reliants*. In that first "experimental" year All American's crews retrieved/dropped-off some 75,000 pounds of airmail and 6,500 pounds of air express, averaging 78 "pickups" per day for a 94-percent completion rate.

But All American found itself caught in the usual inter-agency Washington squabbling. Postmaster General Farley had recommended that the service be continued past the one-year cutoff, but the Civil Aeronautics Authority (to become the C.A.B) ruled that, as long as the Experimental Airmail Act existed, it had no jurisdiction over mail delivery and thus could not issue a Certificate of Public Convenience and Necessity. It took Congressional legislation, signed into law on July 5, 1940, to kill the Experimental Airmail Act and transfer jurisdiction of Pick-up Mail to the CAA. On July 22 All American received its Certificate to operate Airmail Route 49, actually five separate routes which would eventually serve more than 105 communities. Technically, All American's 1940 authorization makes it the first local to be certificated, beating out even the revived Essair (above).

But All American was still not carrying passengers. Washington had ruled that this was a mail-and-packages-only route, and that no passengers could be transported aboard those Stinsons. In December, 1944, five months from the official date of Docket 857, All American asked that it be allowed to carry passengers between some of the larger cities on some routes. Four years passed until, in 1948, the C.A.B. agreed that All American could carry mail, express, and passengers into 25 cities on six route segments comprising Airmail Route 97.

The company began its first passenger service on March 7, 1949, using DC-3s. Its new home base was Washington, D.C. and its new name was All American Airways. Officially a passenger/mail/freight operation, it operated its last pick-up mail service in July of 1949. In

1953 it would again change its name, to Allegheny Airways, honoring that mid-Atlantic region of its birth.

10. Southern – June 10, 1949 :

For a paper airline it certainly had some big plans. In its application it proposed hundreds of miles of routes connecting New Orleans, Louisiana with Raleigh-Durham, Miami with Nashville, Tampa with Charlotte, etc. Big plans indeed for a would-be airline that had not yet purchased its first airplane.

But Southern's president, Frank W. Hulse, dreamed big. Southern Airways of Georgia, the FBO-cum-flight school that he and partner Ike Jones had purchased in 1936, already was a fixture at ten airports in three states and would go on to become the internationally-known Hangar One. Next would come an airline. Hulse chartered Southern Airways, Inc. on July 7, 1943, and on January 6, 1944, applied for certification.

It lost the first round. On March 28, 1946 the C.A.B.'s Florida Case awarded the routes between New Orleans and most of Florida to Orlando Airlines, later renamed Florida Airways. Eastern Air Lines and National Airlines, both of which viewed Florida as their private turf., had protested, and the C.A.B. had listened.

But Southern was by no means out of the running. A year later, on April 4, 1947 the C.A.B. announced its findings in the Southeastern States Case, awarding to Southern a complex system covering 1,340 miles serving 23 cities in seven southeastern states.

The would-be airline had its first route system; what it didn't have was the cash to begin service – nor anything resembling a fleet. Its one airplane was a refurbished C-47B/DC-3 purchased in 1946 from the Reclamation Finance Corporation. Hulse set out to raise working capital, but soon discovered that in the late 1940s airlines were out of favor with investors. While he scrambled for funding he raised some money by leasing that sole airplane to Piedmont. Finding investors was only half of his problem. The C.A.B. was inviting comment on Southern's route awards in the Mississippi Valley Case, announced December 18, 1947. Four established airlines – Delta, Chicago & Southern, Eastern, and National – plus a bus company, Continental Southern Lines, all voiced objections; the regional bus operator claimed local transportation should be by bus only.

Finally in late 1948, with a capitalization bankroll of $300,000, Hulse petitioned the C.A.B. for the delayed certification. He got the certificate effective February 8, 1949 and planned to start operations that June.

But there was a last-minute challenge by Florida Airways, which first argued that it deserved Southern's routes, as the latter was obviously a late-starter, and, when that didn't work, demanded to merge with Southern. The C.A.B. denied the request in April 1949.

By the end of May Southern had a five-airplane fleet: the original DC-3, now back from Piedmont, plus four others. Service was to begin June 10, 1949. But June in the South comes in two varieties: 'humid, hot, and clear' or 'humid, hot, rainy, and sometimes foggy.' It was fog that prevailed that June morning as Southern Flight 1 waited to start its Atlanta – Gadsden – Birmingham – Tuscaloosa – Columbus

– Memphis round trip. Hulse had delayed the departure, claiming even the birds were walking.

Then the C.A.B. called to tell him it was now or never – his certificate was toast if he didn't start service immediately. Hulse gave the go-ahead, and the flight finally departed, marking the start of 30 years of consistent service to the South.

11. Central - September 15, 1949 :

Southern Flight (later *Flight* magazine) called Central's fleet of Beechcraft Bonanzas "airliners-in-miniature." Beginning service on September 15, 1949 (certification was November 14, 1946) with a fleet of 11 Bonanzas, Central was taking advantage of a 1949 C.A.B. ruling allowing single-engine aircraft. Without that decision Central might have remained a paper airline.

Founder Keith Kahle, a former oil-field worker turned aviation-writer turned flying school operator was having trouble getting the funding to begin operations. His three-year temporary certificate was about to elapse when along came the C.A.B.'s ruling. Instead of the estimated one million dollars needed for DC-3s he was able to purchase a fleet of Beech Bonanzas for one-quarter of that total. Central's Flight One departed from Fort Worth for Oklahoma City via five intermediate stops.

From that September 15 start date the Bonanzas and their uniformed pilots were kept busy shuttling around a five-segment route system that stretched from Ft. Worth as far north as Wichita, Kansas. But not after sunset. The four-seaters, with a useful load of 600 pounds (not including the pilot) had no advanced instrumentation and seldom exceeded 145 mph at a 2,500 foot altitude. Actually the airline was IFR – classic IFR, or "I Follow Roads." Years later one pilot reminisced in *The Central Skywriter*, a company newsletter, "We only had to worry about (colliding with) our own flights because other planes would be either high above us on instrument clearance – or waiting it out on the ground."

There were 23 cities on that early route map, ranging from recognized cities like Dallas or Tulsa to 'where-is-that?' towns like Oklahoma's Shawnee or Ada. But already Kahle and his staff were looking for suitable twin-engine equipment, at one point considering the de Havilland Dove. By late 1950 Central would operate DC-3s, no different from its counterparts. Fifteen years later it would be the first to add the Convair 600, a Rolls Royce Dart-powered retrofit of the Convair 240, and its route map would include 41 destinations in six states.

12. Lake Central - November 13, 1949 :

One of the smaller carriers, Lake Central is notable, first, for its flamboyant founder and, second, because it became the only employee-owned local. "Colonel" Roscoe Turner, three-time winner of the Thompson Trophy and self-promoting showman famed for traveling about with pet lion, Gilmore, started the airline as "Turner Airlines – The Lake Central Route," basing it in Indianapolis, Indiana, which Turner thought of as a hub of air transport.

In 1940 he and some colleagues had begun the Roscoe Turner Aeronautical Corporation in Indianapolis, kept alive by wartime government contracts. Early in 1947 he applied for a certificate to offer service from Indianapolis to ten heartland destinations in Indiana and four other states, using two DC-3s and three Beech Bonanzas. Although they got the C.A.B. certificate on September 3, 1947, there wasn't enough money to start service. On May 31, 1949, the company formed Turner Airlines, Inc. Turner sold a 75-percent interest in the company to John and Paul Weesner from Nebraska, who also owned Nationwide Air Transport Service. In exchange Turner Airlines received the needed working capital and four DC-3s. Service began on November 11, 1949 with a DC-3 route from Indianapolis to Grand Rapids, Michigan via Kokomo and South Bend, Indiana and Kalamzoo, Michigan.

The airline had to purchase single-engine Beech Bonanzas to service cities such as Connersville and Lafayette, Indiana, whose airports were so primitive they could not handle a "large" airplane like the DC-3. Those Bonanzas would serve as late as 1952, when Connersville was dropped and Lafayette upgraded its field to DC-3 standards. Early on, in December 1950, the stockholders voted to change the name to Lake Central Airlines.

By 1952 Turner sought to sell his interest. Meanwhile North Central Airlines had acquired a controlling interest of Lake Central stock and was looking to merge the two airlines. Since a merger would require C.A.B. approval, the stock was placed in trust, where it remained for two years while the C.A.B. attended to other matters.

Weary of the delay, North Central voted to sell out to a group of Lake Central officers and employees,. In January 1955, 65-percent of the Lake Central work force purchased an average 500 shares apiece. But they still were not the real owners, as the C.A.B. had yet to rule on the North Central merger request. Finally, in June 1957, it unanimously rejected North Central's bid. A North Central appeal took another two years to resolve. Finally, in June of 1959, Lake Central became the first employee-owned airline.

13. Bonanza – December 19, 1949 :

To a miner of precious metals, a "bonanza" mans "a rich vein or pocket of ore"; to a gambler it iseans a "jackpot, winning streak, luck"' and to residents of Las Vegas and Reno, Nevada it meant, as of August 6, 1946, a faster way to travel between the two cities, some 344 miles apart.

The plucky little airline began with just one airplane, a four-passenger Cessna 195, with which it had begun offering charter trips in June 1945 as Bonanza Air Services. Business was good, and on December 31, 1945, it incorporated as a charter service and flight school. Besides the Cessna 195, the fleet would now include two Piper Cubs, three ex-military Cessna T-50 Bobcats, and an open-cockpit Stearman biplane for pilot training. Then, in early 1946 Bonanza won a contract to ferry merchant sailors from neighboring California to the

East Coast. Now it was time to obtain a "real" airliner – a converted C-47 leased from the War Assets Administration in March 1946. A month later that airplane made its first flight for the now-renamed Bonanza Air Lines, Inc., which was about to hit another lucky break.

A railway strike created tremendous demand for on-demand air charter, and the surge of business convinced the three founders – Ed Converse, June Simon, and Charlie Keene – that there was sufficient demand to sustain an intrastate airline. That August, 1946 flight marked the start of a truly bizarre schedule, with the sole airplane making one northbound or southbound flight per weekday. Weekends were for maintenance or, if the fates smiled, for weekend charter trips, which helped pay the bills in that first lean year.

The lean times became leaner as passenger boardings sank. Then, to Bonanza's rescue came the Las Vegas and Reno Chambers of Commerce, which agreed to allocate $10,000 for an advertising campaign aimed at boosting travel between the two gambling meccas. Gradually the campaign proved successful. Bonanza acquired a second airplane, an ex-Western Air Lines DC-3, and by September 1947 was offering daily roundtrips between the two cities. It had also applied for C.A.B. certification as a local.

It took almost two years, but on June 15, 1949, the C.A.B. finally awarded Bonanza the right to operate its route as a mail-, express-, and passenger-carrying airline. Five months later it approved the transfer of TWA's Las Vegas – Phoenix segment, giving Bonanza true interstate status. The official start as a scheduled local service airline came a month later, on December 19, 1949. Within a few years Bonanza's DC-3s, with a big "B" emblazoned on a bold orange tail, would become a familiar feature across the desert southwest and along the southern California coast. By the close of 1959 the fleet would include six Fairchild F-27A turboprops, and a year later the last DC-3 would be retired amidst great hoopla, with six-airplane Bonanza proclaiming itself the "First all jet-powered airline in America!"

14. Ozark – September 26, 1950 :

The second youngest of all locals proves the adage "all things come to those who wait." And quite a wait it was.

Several months after Lindbergh's 1927 flight, Oliver L. Parks established, in the city of St. Louis, Missouri, a school to teach aircraft design and maintenance. Parks Air College became the first federally-certified school of aeronautics, training some ten percent of all new World War II pilots and mechanics. After the war, Parks sold his college to Saint Louis University, created Parks Air Transport, and applied for certification as a local service airline. His reputation helped convince the C.A.B. that Parks was the most fit, willing, and able of all the applicants., In December, 1947, the agency awarded it a 3,000-mile complex of routes centered on St. Louis, with service expected to begin shortly thereafter.

The expectations proved premature. Despite a stellar reputation, Parks was a bit short in capital and kept postponing the start of service on most of its assigned routes. That's when a group of local businessmen stepped up. Two years earlier Homer Dale "Laddie" Hamilton and his three partners had also applied for certification as a local. To demonstrate that they were fit, willing, and able to operate an airline they had invested in three Beech Staggerwings and on January 10, 1945, began an intrastate service between Springfield, St. Louis, and Kansas City, Missouri. The operation lasted less than a year. Nothing was happening with their C.A.B. application and their original Ozark Air Lines, offering two-flights-per-day, was in the red.

Eventually the C.A.B., aware that Parks was yet to start operations, reopened hearings. On July 28, 1950, the agency awarded Parks's routes to Hamilton's Ozark Air Lines and to Mid-Continent Airlines (later absorbed by Braniff). Ozark acquired four of Parks's DC-3s, and on September 26, 1950, an Ozark DC-3 departed on a St. Louis – Chicago flight, with three intermediate stops. The sole passenger had the airplane to himself. But the cabins wouldn't stay empty for long. In 1951 Ozark would carry some 53,000 passengers.

By 1959 Ozark was servicing 52 cities in ten states with a fleet of 24 DC-3s and three Fokker F-27 *Friendship* turboprops. It was with the introduction of those airplanes that the "three swallows" logo first appeared. But no matter what the logo, the local that didn't begin service until 1950 – the year that also marked the start of the conflict in Korea – was well on its way.

15. Air New England - January 20, 1975 :

If the locals were considered the "second level" of U.S. domestic airline service, then Air New England's founder entered the airline business even further down the food chain, as a "third level" or "scheduled air taxi operator." Joseph C. (Joe) Whitney was a 28-year-old former employee of both Slick Airways and Northeast Airlines. In 1959 he formed National Executive Flight Service, a scheduled air taxi operation with a fleet of two twin- and three single-engine airplanes, and began service on June 20, 1960. By 1969 Whitney's Executive Airlines, spun off from National Executive Flight Service, had a fleet of ten Beech 99s and eight de Havilland Canada Twin Otters and won *Air Transport World*'s "Commuter Airline of the Year" accolade. A year later, unable to tolerate the airline's new owner, Whitney resigned as president. But by November 1970 he was back in the business. His backers helped him acquire the fleet and route certificate of the defunct Cape and Islands Air Service, creating Air New England. The new airline's first trip left Massachusetts' Nantucket Island at 0700 on November 15, 1970, for a day that would include some 16 landings and takeoffs.

Eighteen months later the fleet numbered four ex- trunk airline DC3s, and Whitney had begun petitioning the C.A.B. for certification as a local service operator, sensing that the ailing Northeast would have trouble serving the smaller communities of the region from which it took its name. On August 1, 1972 Northeast formally disappeared, acquired by Delta Air Lines, which then dropped all of the old Northeast cities except for Maine's Portland and Bangor and Vermont's Burlington. It also sold Whitney six Fairchild FH-227s. By the fourth quarter of 1974 Air New England was ranked second of the 160 U.S. commuter airlines; and on October 15, 1974 the C.A.B., once again besieged by area Congressmen to improve air service to local communities, granted Air New England status as a local service airline, effective January 20, 1975.

It was the first new airline to be certificated in 25 years, and the first commuter to be certificated as a subsidy-eligible local. Although it was short-lived, its airplanes' bold tail stripes of pink/orange/lime/blue brightened drab airport ramps around the Northeast for several years.

Short Flights

Throughout we focus mainly on the thirteen local service airlines receiving permanent certification in 1955, plus pioneering Pioneer and late-blooming Air New England. But there were others. Some would exist only on paper while others did begin operations but lasted a relatively short time. In the interests of historical accuracy, here are brief summaries of their passing.

Monarch, Challenger, and Arizona – see Frontier above

Empire Air Lines – Notable for its early use of the legendary Boeing 247-D, called the first truly modern airliner. Empire began life as the eponymous Zimmerly Air Lines, an Idaho-based intrastate carrier started by Mr. Bert Zimmerly. Service with Cessna aircraft began between Boise and Lewiston, Idaho in June 1944. In 1945 Zimmerly obtained five Boeing 247-Ds from Canadian Pacific Air Lines. In March of 1946 it changed its name to Empire Air Lines, received its feeder certification in May, and began actual service in September of that year. By March, 1948 it was replacing the 247-Ds with DC-3s, and it's routes now stretched westward to include both Spokane and Seattle, Washington plus Portland, Oregon. All of these were cities served by West Coast, and thus it became a logical takeover target. West Coast Airlines absorbed Empire on August 4, 1952.

Mid-West Airlines – This Des Moines-based company began as the Iowa Airplane Company, a fixed base operator, in 1933. Although it received three routes as part of 1946's North Central Case, three years would elapse before it could begin operations, on November 12, 1949. By then it had changed its name to Mid-West and acquired a fleet of seven four-place Cessna 190s. By 1951 the airline's routes touched parts of four states: Iowa, Minnesota, Nebraska, and South Dakota. In November 1951 it was acquired by the Purdue Research Foundation. Although Purdue had also acquired some DC-3s, service never began and, by May 1952 all operations were terminated.

E. W. Wiggins Airways – Yet another example of an airline operator naming his company for himself, but this time the name proved a jinx. In June 1946, he won certification as a local in the New England Case. But the route, which included 22 communities between Albany, the New York state capital, and Boston, Massachusetts, was a disappointment, as Wiggins had hoped to serve New York City. Then financial problems came along. With just six months left on the three-year temporary certificate, Wiggins had yet to start operations. He finally scraped together a fleet of Cessna T-50 Bobcats, and the operation limped along, still under some sort of jinx. The Board denied Wiggins' request to purchase twin-engine de Havilland Doves and began hinting that perhaps the struggling airline call it quits. On August 1, 1953, the C.A.B. terminated the certificate (technically already expired) and awarded the routes to both Mohawk and Northeast.

Florida Airways – The Florida Case, decided on March 28, 1946, awarded to Orlando Airlines (later Florida Airways, Inc.) routes that Southern Airways had sought. Almost a year later Orlando/Florida began Orlando – Jacksonville and Orlando – Tallahassee service with Beech 18s. But this was turf jealously protected by both National and Eastern, and the C.A.B. had allowed Eastern to serve Gainesville and Ocala on its Atlanta – Orlando run. It was just one of the reasons that Florida kept requesting more subsidy to cover its growing losses – so large that the C.A.B. finally ran out of patience and informed Florida that as of March 28, 1949, its certificate would be terminated.

Florida responded by demanding Southern's Route 98, on which the financially-strapped start-up had yet to begin service (see " Southern Airways" above). When Southern replied by saying it would begin service shortly, Florida tried another tack. It asked the C.A.B. to arrange a shotgun-wedding between itself and Southern, claiming that there had been a tentative engagement from which Southern had bolted and now would not answer the phone. The C.A.B. remained skeptical and in mid-April 1949 said there would be no arranged marriage. With its last recourse gone, so was Florida.

Aborted Takeoffs

A brief listing of planned local service airlines which never actually began service:

Parks Air Transport – Certificated in December 1947 – planned to serve Missouri and Illinois – certificate canceled on July 28, 1950, and routes given to both Ozark and Mid-Continent (see " Ozark" above)

Yellow Cab Company of Cleveland – Certificated September 1947 – Certificate canceled March 1951.

Island Air Ferries – Certificated February 1948 to serve New York and Long island area but never operated .

Air Commuting – Certificated May 1947 – Canceled November 1950

Purdue Aeronautics Corp. – Certificated 1949 – Certificate expired January 30, 1950, when Turner (Lake Central) began service.

Now that we know how each of the Locals began, lets take a look at the very early struggles of these 'new kids on the block' to attract passengers and survive.

Chapter 3: A Long Slow Climb

Some, especially those who revere prop-liners, call the 1950s 'The Golden Age' of U.S. commercial aviation – and with good reason. By the start of the decade four-engine airliners were not uncommon. Lockheed's "Connies" (*Constellations*) and Douglas's DC-4s had been in trans-continental service since 1946 and the new DC-6 since 1947. As the 50s progressed aviation buffs could delight in the introduction of the DC-7, the *Super Constellation*, the *Stratocruiser*, the Convair 340/440, and the Martin 4-0-4. And on the horizon were turboprops and even pure jets.

From the airline accountant's perspective there was also good news. In the five years since the close of WWII, passenger-mile traffic had trebled, partially a result of a new air-mindedness but more the product of new coach fares, as well as larger aircraft, more non-stop routes, and higher frequencies as the airlines added equipment. By 1950 the airlines had surpassed the railroads as the dominant inter-city carrier. As Davies writes in *Airlines of the United States Since 1914*, the airlines "had gained new stature, respect, and recognition."

Somehow that stature, respect, and recognition had so far eluded the local service airlines. They were the new kids on the block – and they weren't impressing the neighbors. Even their supporters were having some doubts. The Locals' biggest booster, a veritable one-man cheering squad, was the late George Haddaway, editor of the respected

Flight magazine. In a 1950 editorial he admitted that, up till that point, he too had been wondering if this C.A.B. experiment would ever work out.

One reason was that the locals were having an image problem: their equipment was outdated, in some cases relatively ancient; they had no name-recognition; and they were competing with other, more established, forms of short-haul transportation, such as the Midwest's network of Interurban Rail Cars that plagued Lake Central in its early years (ironically, Lake Central once marketed itself as "The Flying Interurban").

In the long view, however, things were not so bad as some suggested. By mid-1950, 16 locals operated some 30,000 miles of routes in every region of the U.S. In 1945 there had been only one – Essair – operating its skimpy route across Texas. In 1945 it boarded just 4,450 passengers; in 1949, renamed Pioneer, it boarded 23 times as many (104,110, to be exact). For the first half of 1950 the feeders as a group had boarded 388,000 passengers, producing revenues of $4.3 million. All American, just 16 months into its passenger-carrying identity, had posted more in passenger revenues (nearly $354,00) for the second fiscal quarter of 1950 than the total revenue for all locals for all of 1945.

To executives of the trunk airlines those revenue numbers probably seemed laughable. But the locals could not be measured by trunk airline standards, for their role was very different. A comparison of 'Points Served' with 'Points Served Exclusively' reveals their uniqueness. From 22- to 68-percent of their destinations had no other form of scheduled airline service. The local was the only show in town – which was exactly what the C.A.B. had had in mind.

Defending that C.A.B. thinking, one writer used the analogy of the hare versus the hound, claiming that the Board instinctively understood why the former always outruns the latter. The routes given to the locals had such "limited traffic potential" that only a special breed of entrepreneur could make any money serving them. The locals were thus like the hare. They ran to stay alive while the hound (the trunks) was merely "running for ... lunch." And the history of those early years shows that the locals did indeed run, and run very hard. Not that they were running from the trunks, for the C.A.B. protected them from such competition, but they were running just to stay alive.

Which was not so easy. The locals serviced 343 communities, and the average daily boardings at the start of the 1950s numbered just a half-dozen. True, some places boarded twice as many, but others boarded only one or two passengers per day. Little wonder why that first decade was such a struggle to survive, and why everyone – from flight crews to station agents – had to pitch in.

For example, in addition to their regular airport duties (selling tickets, loading baggage, checking the weather) Southern's station managers were expected to make sales calls, as many as 800 per month, to local businesses and civic groups. Pilots were also recruited to talk to school groups, and to meet with local media outlets, offering to barter trips for advertising. A June 1957 photo in *Flight* shows some Southern 'stews,' in 50's-era pillbox caps, at an Atlanta supermarket promotion featuring free trips to a Florida beach town. Another photo showed Southern's President Frank W. Hulse in a television studio, dressed in a cowboy hat and checkered sport jacket and awkwardly holding a rifle.

Central focused on increasing its revenue from mail pay without mailing bricks, as some disreputable types at some trunk airlines had done in the bad old days. Using the slogan "If a letter is worth writing it is worth an air mail stamp," the local recruited 200 school-age children from Ardmore, Oklahoma (population 17,900) to go door-to-door distributing air mail stickers and schedules. The reward was coupons for free merchandise from local stores. Soon the postmaster was reporting a 67-percent increase in airmail usage, and Central happily repeated the contest in other Oklahoma communities.

Frontier also worked with individual communities, literally blitzing a town with an "Air Week." From Monday through Saturday Frontier's sales staff would visit key players such as the local Chamber of Commerce, the local newspaper, etc. to promote air travel for the businessman. Then on Sunday two DC-3s filled with Frontier staff plus media people arrived from Denver. All the advance publicity, plus displays of Air National Guard and Air Force equipment, would attract hundreds of local residents out to the airport. As in the old barnstormer era, Frontier offered 20-minute sightseeing flights, hoping that many of these first-time fliers would become future passengers.

Also barnstorming was Pioneer, which offered 10- to 15-minute sample "hops" and even gave away Buffalo Nickels, appropriate because its logo depicted an American Buffalo. Pioneer also relied on another bit of Americana – the radio jingle. In 1954 it launched its "Travel in Style / For Just Pennies per Mile!" ad campaign, whose commercials all ended with "When it's far by car / It's near by Pioneer! / and the sound of a radial-engine airplane droning overhead.

For Pioneer, unfortunately, even a dozen upbeat jingles could not have solved its financial troubles, and on April 1, 1955 it was absorbed by Continental, ironically 'pioneering' in another sense as the first operational local service airline to be acquired by another carrier (see Chapter 10, "Off the Radar Scope"). Some argue that the airline's financial crisis was the direct result of the C.A.B. ruling against its acquisition of Martin 2-0-2s (see Chapter 4, "A Change of Planes"). Although that argument is not without merit, it flies against conventional wisdom. Generally the C.A.B. protected these fledglings in many ways, including protection from destructive competition by the larger carriers. Without that safeguard they might never have survived.

But they did survive, and by the mid-1950s they were almost ready to be removed from the endangered species list. According to one contemporary publication, the number of revenue passengers carried by the locals tripled between 1950 and 1955 while airmail and express ton-miles were up more than double and freight ton-miles had almost doubled. These admittedly second-level carriers, whom *Business Week* magazine had once derided as "small potatoes," were beginning to grab some traction.

And good news for these airlines also translated into good news for the communities they served. "Has airline service resulted in the location of new industry in your community?" was a question that Southern Airways in 1955 asked the Chambers of Commerce of the communities for which it was the sole air transport provider. The response was overwhelmingly positive, with nearly all replying that the new industries would never have come there had there been no regularly scheduled airline service.

Take relatively rural Kingman, Arizona (pop. 18,000) in the northwestern part of the state some 160 miles (258 km) from Phoenix. It attracted a Ford Motor Company proving ground simply because Bonanza served that city. And across the country the famed Zippo cigarette lighter company, in Bradford, Pennsylvania, thrived because of the easy access provided by Allegheny, even though the woodsy town is far from any railroads or waterways. In fact, Allegheny Airlines was credited with helping to bring no fewer than "28 new industries into the Wilkes-Barre/Scranton, Pennsylvania area," as American Airlines noted in its 1965 tribute: How Local Airlines Put Main Street on the Map.

Main Street began to take notice. Stories began appearing, even in mass-market publications, touting the benefits of the new airline service provided by the locals. Often the communities worked hard to attract and keep that all-important air service. Grateful for Bonanza's finally linking the northern and southern parts of Nevada, the city of Reno donated a surplus hangar for that airline to use at its Las Vegas base, dismantling and trucking the structure some 500 miles south. One community was so glad to have Ozark provide airline service that it waived all rent, utility charges, and landing fees for the first six months of operation and donated $500 to furnish the terminal. Other cities modernized their airports by constructing terminal buildings and lengthening runways. To lure service by Central Airlines, the city of Fayetteville, Arkansas essentially remade its Drake Field in 1955.

That year, 1955, holds special significance in the annals of the local service airlines. It was the year that they shed the stigma of impermanence and took their place as part of the nation's transportation system. On May 19, 1955, President Dwight D. Eisenhower signed legislation effectively ordering the C.A.B. to grant permanent certification to the locals. Their temporary or experimental role was ended, and this, some suggest, was as significant for the well-being of the locals as 1938's Civil Aeronautics Act had been for the trunk airlines.

Until Permanent Certification, the locals' Certificates of Public Convenience and Necessity had been only temporary, subject to periodic review. Although this was exactly what the ever-cautious C.A.B. had thought would protect the tax-payer from inefficient operators, it had the same effect as tying lead weights to a swimmer's legs – it just held back the locals. Haddaway explained that the temporary status discouraged investors, which meant a lack of working capital to acquire more up-to-date equipment. Secondly it made management's job more difficult, as every few years they had to assemble all the documentation required by the C.A.B. for its renewal hearings. And the C.A.B.'s bureaucratic slowness meant that approval could waste months. One witness at the Senate hearings into permanent certification gave as an example Ozark. Their original certificate expired in September, 1953, but even though the airline would receive a five-year renewal, to expire September, 1958, it took the C.A.B. until early 1955 to announce that decision. Which meant that for 18 months Ozark was in a kind of certification limbo.

The law that amended Section 401 (e) of the 1938 Civil Aeronautics Act eliminated forever such situations by authorizing certificates "of permanent duration" to these struggling carriers. Two-and-one-quarter years later another piece of legislation would provide an equally significant boost.

Commonly known as The Guaranteed Loan Act, this law, passed on September 7, 1957, directed the C.A.B. to guarantee private lenders against any loss on a loan not just to the local service airlines but to metropolitan helicopter airlines and territorial airlines. The Act, originally written to cover the five-year period 1957 – 1962 and later renewed, guaranteed up to $5 million to any one airline for the purchase of new equipment, and protected lenders for up to 90percent of the amount lent.

For the locals this was great news, for it meant that they could begin – or at least begin to consider – an image makeover. For years the locals' CEOs had moaned about their outdated equipment. The DC-3 was ill-suited to short trips, was costly to operate, and was, in the eyes of all but aviation buffs, just plain old. Now the locals had a real opportunity to shed their ancient pelicans and acquire the airliners that would appeal to the public.

As we'll see in a later chapter, West Coast began F-27 service on September 27, 1958. Piedmont followed in November of that year, and they were in turn followed by Bonanza (March, 1959), Pacific (April, 1959), and Ozark (September, 1959). Turboprops were then new (in fact, Eastern's Lockheed Electras didn't start service until January 12, 1959) and this modern equipment had a positive effect. Bonanza, for example, reported double the number of boardings for its F-27A *Silver Darts* over its DC-3s in the Las Vegas – Phoenix market.

What a difference a decade makes. By the end of the 1950s the local service airlines were looking a lot healthier than they had ten years earlier. It had been a struggle, and although Pioneer had not made it, the others were definitely on their way. And now it was time to think about acquiring some more up-to-date airplanes.

Chapter 4: A Change of Planes

For most of the 1950s the local service airlines were known, for better or worse, as DC-3 operators. But the honest truth is that continuing to rely on the DC-3 was a money-losing prospect. Originally it had seemed a good choice for these startups: available at reasonable prices, it gave the image of a 'modern' airliner (as opposed to a Lockheed L-10A or other out-moded type).

But the DC-3 was never meant to be a short-hop airliner, and using it in that mode proved costly. In *Airlines of the U.S. Since 1914*, Davies notes that just to pay for the crew costs, a DC-3 would have had to have at least three of its seats filled every flight, and that was just one of its many fixed expenses. An Aviation Week article noted that even at a 65% load factor the DC-3 would still yield passenger revenues of only .82 cents per mile, far short of the $1.00 per mile minimum operating cost. In other words, for every mile flown, the DC-3 was losing money, even if it were two-thirds full.

And sometimes, by the second half of the 1950s, passenger loads exceeded seating capacity. Piedmont's President Davis noted, "...the saturation load factor on an annual basis for the typical local service airline is on the order of 55 to 60%. When load factors higher than this are realized a lot of passengers are being turned away, especially on peak traffic days. Under such conditions a carrier is not rendering good service to the public." Nor was Davis alone in his assessment;

two other local service airline presidents – Mohawk's Robert E. Peach and Allegheny's Leslie

O. Barnes – had already noted that problem several years earlier, in two magazine articles. In 1954 Mohawk was breaking records for local service load factors – and this was causing some problems. They had already made their DC-3s into 28-seaters, but that solution worked only sometimes. When fueled according to the requirements for instrument weather flying, a 28-seat DC-3 was uncomfortably close to its gross load limits, meaning they had to reduce passenger load. Some 15% of the time the 27th and 28th seats had to remain empty, which meant either disappointing passengers or operating a costly one-way extra section. And this was happening with increasing frequency. Peach claimed that 28 times in one week Mohawk's load factors equaled 70 percent and the company had had to operate 16 extra sections.

In his article, Allegheny's president corroborated Peach's analysis of the DC-3's problems. His airline was also having to turn away passengers more often. Average load factors were exceeding 60 percent, and some segments, even those with three intermediate stops, were averaging 70- to 75-percent. As he saw it, there were two possible alternatives. "Should the situation," he wrote, "be met with two DC3s, with two crews, two operations and two schedules or should it be met with larger equipment?"

Actually this was a rhetorical question, for both Mohawk and Allegheny had already committed to new equipment – the articles were written to justify the bold move, and possibly to boast. Peach was exceedingly proud of the three Convair 240s about to join his fleet.

Locating them, he wrote, was an extreme stroke of good fortune, since at an average 250 hours of flight time apiece they were relatively low-mileage. Even though they were international travelers. The three, serial numbers 100, 127, and 129 on the Convair production line, were part of a batch of six 240-14s built early in 1949, delivered to Central Air Transport Corp., and then purchased by General Claire Chenault's Civil Air Transport, Inc. in mid-December of that year. But they ran afoul of the People's Republic of China and spent several years parked in Hong Kong. Legal wrangling finally secured CAT the right to reclaim five of them, which, according to Peach's account, were shipped back to Convair for inspection and storage.

Two were purchased by oil companies, but Mohawk optioned the remaining three, although it was nearly outbid by the government of Pakistan before the C.A.B. expedited approval for purchase. They joined the Mohawk fleet as *Air Chief Oneida*, *Air Chief Nanticoke*, and *Air Chief Seneca*.

Mohawk's accountants probably suffered 'sticker-shock" when they realized the final price. Peach himself noted that the $1.1M cost was the airline's most extensive financial undertaking to date. It included the $300,000 per aircraft cost, plus another $115,000 for spare engines, parts, radios, etc. But, according to Peach, it was worth it. Although the new airplanes' hourly operating costs were triple the costs for a DC-3, the larger and faster airplanes would produce much better hourly revenues than the DC-3, thus justifying their purchase. What it all meant, Peach insisted, was that the Convairs would ensure that "7,200 additional passengers will have Mohawk seats available to them at the time they wish to travel." To accomplish this with DC-3s, he added, would have meant buying three more of the dowagers, in addition to the two they had been considering when they located their Convairs.

To obtain necessary financing, Mohawk first had to reduce outstanding debt to Chase Manhattan Bank's satisfaction. One step was to sell off its Sikorsky S-55 helicopter, which had given them bragging rights as the sole local with helicopter service, even though that service lasted only four months in the summer of 1955. They also sold additional shares of company stock, most of it to backers and employees excited about the new Convairs.

It must have been easy to get excited about the new airplane. Not only was it faster and roomier than the DC-3, but it also had tricycle gear (no more struggling up a sharply canted aisle), plus pressurization and weather radar (no more bouncing through the thunderstorms). And it just looked "modern," an asset that Peach hoped would win over finicky citified business travelers as well as impress leisure travelers. Besides, American Airlines operated the Convair, and, as Peach noted, "in our area the public has already accepted the 240 as standard short-haul equipment on American's schedules."

Mohawk's people labored mightily, and its first Convair service was July 1, 1955 – in time for the Independence Day holiday period. To arouse interest it had run advertisements proclaiming " Mohawk

Convairs Are Coming!" and noting that Mohawk would be the first local to operate post-war equipment with pressurized cabins!" The three words "with pressurized cabins" made Mohawk top-dog. Out in California, Southwest's newly-acquired Martin 2-0-2's, meant to replace/supplant its DC-3s, were not pressurized. Ironically it was the ill-fated Pioneer that was the first local to replace DC-3s with Martins. But that proved to be a fatal move. Although just about everyone acknowledged that the locals needed to find a replacement for their DC-3s, the C.A.B. was not quite ready to sign off on any local's independent initiative. The story was originally told to the U.S. House of Representatives, during hearings on permanent certification, by Branifff Airways' future president, Harding L. Lawrence, who was then a Pioneer vice-president.

According to Lawrence, Pioneer, like other locals, was definitely beginning to outgrow its DC-3s. Already in 1951 it had realized a 26-percent growth in passenger boardings, and management was convinced that a larger and faster airplane could allow the airline to gain "complete self-sufficiency" and eventually become subsidy-free. They had considered several possible candidates, including the Super DC-3, the SAAB Scandia, and the Convair 340, which they actually ordered for 1954 delivery, but lost because of Korean War production priorities. After a proposed deal with TWA for nine of its 2-0-2As fell through, all Pioneer could obtain were nine ex-Northwest 2-0-2s, an older version that had a reputation as being somewhat snakebit.

The Martin 2-0-2 had first entered service with Northwest almost five years earlier, in late 1947, but then suffered an embarrassing run of mishaps and accidents. Things became so bad that Northwest pilots refused to fly any unmodified Martin 2-0-2 after March 17, 1951. So Northwest simply grounded all of them. But it still retained ownership, and so transferred 12 airplanes to charter and non-scheduled operator Transocean Air Lines, where they had a varied and checkered history, including two more fatal accidents, until Pioneer came along as a purchaser.

The purchase price of the airplanes, plus overhaul and modification, came to $4.1M. But Pioneer thought it found a way to ease the bite. It happily sold eleven of its DC-3s to the U.S. Air Force, actually earning a profit of $841K, which it used to offset losses on mail subsidies. The 2-0-2s entered service in June, 1952 as *Pacemasters* (not to be confused with Piedmont's *Pacemakers*). Each 2-0-2 was named for a legendary Texan, such as *Pacemaster Kit Carson*. Then came a major tactical error

– Pioneer applied for an increased rate of mail pay to defray the costs associated with the new airplanes.

It took them ten months, but in its Pioneer Mail Rate Decision the C.A.B. emphatically said 'No Deal!' Pioneer, it said, was to receive mail pay at DC-3 rates, even though it had racked up ten months of extra expenses operating the Martins. Why? First of all, this was not the "economical and efficient management" required by statute. Secondly, the Martin "was tailored to trunk-line requirements" and was not meant for a local air service system." Thus it would be a mistake to "pour money" into the support of a Martin 2-0-2 operation, the Board argued, because they would not "be advancing one step further" towards the goal of finding the ideal local service aircraft.

Some cynics accused the C.A.B. of a hidden agenda – that it did not want a local to have modern equipment that could compete with that operated by established trunks Continental and Braniff. Others accused it of not wanting small Texas communities to have modern service.

More reasonable souls argued that there was some validity to the C.A.B.'s decision. First, the sale of the DC-3s just didn't sit right. The Board was uncomfortable with the idea of an airline making a private profit from equipment that had involved subsidy, or public money. Also the Board was unconvinced that the Martins would actually permit Pioneer to eventually lower its subsidy requests, despite its claims.

And so nothing, not even a written appeal from U.S. Senator Lyndon Baines Johnson (later 36th President of the United States) could reverse the C.A.B. decision. Which left Pioneer in an embarrassing bind. It couldn't operate its 2-0-2s without the increased subsidy and it had sold off its only other airplanes. It had to lease DC-3s.

But it's difficult to make a profit with rented airplanes. And the C.A.B. drove another nail into Pioneer's coffin when it refused to allow Pioneer to claim the DC-3 rental costs as an expense to be offset by subsidy mail pay. The Board basically accused Pioneer of both *hubris* and bad judgment, arguing that its original DC-3s had already been depreciated at public expense. Had it not become too big for its britches, said the C.A.B., Pioneer would still be operating fully depreciated and wholly-owned airplanes. Therefore, it was not about to make the taxpayers assume additional costs because of management's poor business sense.

By August, 1953 Pioneer was losing $3,000 per day. Seeing an opportunity to kill off a potential competitor, Continental began financial maneuvering, and by December, 1953 a deal had been worked out in which Continental would acquire Pioneer's operating certificate, equipment, etc. The merger was officially consummated on April 1, 1955, some six weeks short of President Eisenhower's signing of the legislation granting permanent status to the locals. Pioneer was gone – possibly because its attempt to modernize could not win the hearts and minds of the C.A.B.

Meanwhile, Southwest's Martin 2-0-2 experience was much more benign. Like Pioneer, it too had obtained its airplanes from Transocean, placing them in service in April, 1953. And it too asked the C.A.B. for increased mail pay, although less than Pioneer had requested. Citing its earlier decision in the Pioneer ruling, the Board again responded in the negative, claiming that increasing mail pay "would not be consistent with the objectives of the Civil Aeronautics Act." But unlike Pioneer, Southwest had not, as the cliché goes, put all its eggs into one basket. Its four 2-0-2s were meant only to supplement DC-3 service, and, the C.A.B.'s Director, Bureau of Air Operations noted that Southwest's "Martin experiment" was a "management responsibility which will not be underwritten with additional mail pay."

He went on to praise the company for seeking private funding and for trying to prove that the Martin "in the limited operations contemplated" can be operated at DC-3 rates, even though he also said that the 2-0-2 was never meant to be a local service airplane. And so, on November 10, 1954 the C.A.B. once again reversed itself, allowing a higher subsidy for Southwest to operate its 2-0-2s. But, the Board warned, their decision was based on Southwest's unique circumstances and was not to be taken as carte blanche approval of such risky attempts at growth.

Eventually Southwest would purchase four more 2-0-2s, from interstate carrier California Central and, ironically, from Pioneer. Then, in November, 1959 Southwest, now calling itself Pacific, exchanged those eight unpressurized 2-0-2s for a similar number of more modern and pressurized Martin 4-0-4s.

So, very gradually, the locals' fleet makeup began changing, although their DC-3s were not about to disappear, not for many years. In 1955 only Allegheny, Mohawk, and Southwest were operating Convairs and Martins. Then, encouraged by two significant pieces of legislation and by the C.A.B.'s apparent willingness to increase subsidy for newer equipment, both North Central and Frontier purchased their first Convairs. The legislation was 1957's Guaranteed Loan Act, or Public Law 85-307, which provided 90%-guaranteed loans of up to $5M per local or territorial airline to buy new equipment, and Public Law 85-295, which encouraged lenders by amending the Federal Bankruptcy Act to provide lender protection similar to that enjoyed by the railroads.

Thus, by the end of 1959, there were 52 Convairs or Martins in the fleets of five locals, that number representing just 17-percent of the entire locals fleet, which also included 220 DC-3s and, as we show further on, 31 turboprops. Over the next six years those percentages would change, although DC-3s would still account for more than one-third of the fleet as late as 1964.

Some observers note that statistics such as these prove the locals were slow to innovate, pointing out that they were nine years behind the trunks in introducing pressurized aircraft (remember, Mohawk's Convairs first entered service on July 1, 1955) and that it took them twice as long (six as opposed to three years) to produce half their Available Seat Miles (ASMs) in pressurized aircraft. Of course such criticism ignores the special circumstances surrounding the locals, their finances, their mandate, etc.

It also ignores the fact that a local adopted turboprop power <u>before</u> some of the trunks did. That local was West Coast, and the airplane was the turboprop Fokker F-27 *Friendship*, which, license-built by Fairchild Engine and Airplane Corporation, became the F-27. Although Capital Airlines had begun Vickers *Viscount* service three years earlier, on July 26, 1955, West Coast would put its twin-engine turboprop into service on September 27, 1958, almost four months <u>before</u> the Lockheed *Electra* would enter service with Eastern Air Lines on January 12, 1959. The F-27 was certainly appealing. With a

270 mph operating speed, the ability to climb to 10,000 feet in seven minutes, and a 4,000-foot take-off distance, the high-wing, pressurized, air-conditioned tricycle-geared 36- to 40-seat seat turboprop seemed the thoroughly-modern answer to the locals' needs.

Joining the bandwagon was Piedmont's president Tom Davis, who was openly gleeful at the prospect. He believed that "the additional seats will produce .84 cents per mile more revenue than the DC-3" and that the turboprop would cost only .36 cents more per mile to operate. "Thus," he concluded, "for only .36 cent per mile increase in operating cost we gain .84 cent per mile in earning ability." And, that potential profit of .48 cents per mile "is substantially greater than our present mail pay."

A firm believer in the F-27, Davis not only saw it as a way for Piedmont to become subsidy-free but he urged the other more successful locals to consider its purchase also. Across the country in Seattle, Nick Bez, President of West Coast Airways, must have read Davis' argument with a broad smile – knowing that he, an émigré from a small fishing village in Yugoslavia, was already ahead of his American-born colleague. West Coast would beat out Piedmont for the accolade of launch customer. Admirers of Bez eagerly retell the story of how a Fairchild salesperson decided to stop by Bez's Seattle office to chat about the new airplane. Painfully aware of the DC-3's shortcomings, Bez listened politely and invited the Fairchild representative to return the next day. "Next morning when that salesman come back, I flobbergost (sic) him. I send him home with a $30,000 option for one of his planes," Bez told a reporter.

West Coast's F-27 service began on September 28, 1958, followed, among the locals, by Piedmont (November, 1958), Bonanza (March, 1959), Pacific (April, 1959), and Ozark (September, 1959). Within a year the airplane was racking-up truly amazing results in passenger boardings.

Take the record accumulated by Bonanza's first three F-27A '*Silver Darts*', for example. The hard-working airplanes operated one daily Las Vegas - Reno roundtrip, three daily Las Vegas - Phoenix trips, and one Phoenix – Salt Lake City trip. And effectively doubled average boardings for April, 1959 compared to 1958. Where the DC-3s on the Phoenix run had been averaging 10.8 boardings per segment, the

Silver Darts were averaging 22.5 a year later. As *Flight* reported, "... where the Silver Dart flights replaced DC-3s Bonanza had an 89.74% increase in revenue passenger miles for 1959 over 1958."

Similar, albeit less spectacular, percentage increases were being recorded by Piedmont, which reported a 45% increase in passengers per plane mile even in the traditionally lean winter months. And besting "Boss Tom's" predictions of "economical" $1.48 per mile costs, Piedmont reported that their F-27s cost just $1.02 per mile. That was .10 cents less than the DC-3's cost and .18 cents less than the average $1.20 per mile cost for a Martin.

Such impressive numbers ignore one basic reality – sticker shock. AvWeek reported that, with accessories, each airplane carried a price tag of $540,000. Thus, someone calculated, had the locals wanted to do a 1-for-1 replacement of DC-3s with F-27s, the total cost would have been $75M. Bonanza was the only local to defy such warnings and do just that. By November, 1960 all of its DC-3s were gone, replaced by F-27As. Its marketing department then cheerfully announced that Bonanza had become the "First All-Jet Airline in the World."

Three locals – Central, Southern, and Trans-Texas – were not exactly boasting about their all-DC-3 fleets as The Fifties came to an end. But they had a reason for sticking with the old girl. As Flight's George Haddaway wrote, "There are many segments where only 8 or 10 passengers will be the loads, and this kind of volume will not justify anything larger than the old DC-3 workhorse." But everyone, even Haddaway, knew there had to be a replacement. Ideally, as the Air Transport Association and the Conference of Local Airlines noted, that would be a 32- to 40-seater capable of at least a 225 mph cruise speed that was also pressurized (for rapid climbs and descents) and could be loaded without special ramp equipment.

For many locals that turned out to be long-in-tooth cast-off Convairs and Martins. One reason, some analysts believe, was the nearly 100 suspensions of short-haul service granted to the trunks between 1959 and 1963, leaving these carriers with un-needed outmoded piston twins. The locals, now serving those former trunk-line destinations, were more than eager to acquire some still perfectly good airplanes. For example, in 1961, when the Board suspended Eastern in favor of Mohawk on many short-haul New England-area routes, Mohawk took over the leases on Eastern's airplanes, acquiring an instant miniature airline.

The second-hand Convairs and Martins did help improve the locals' image and possibly their bottom line, for they were less costly to operate. They also brought a hidden advantage – convertibility – the Convairs, especially, were easily modified as turboprops, as we see in the next chapter.

And so ended the dominance of the DC-3 in the locals' fleets. But the gallant and legendary old girl earns the respect of all who love airplanes. As West Coast wrote about the DC-3 in its 1966 Annual Report:

"She was old, slow, and noisy. But she traversed twenty years and millions of miles for us. The next generation of passengers will know her by reputation only. Her era has ended. But she gave us one magnificent parting gift. She gave us an airline."

But nostalgia doesn't play well in the world of airline economics, and, as we see in the next chapter, it was time to keep modernizing.

Chapter 5: Jet-Propelled

As anyone who lived through it can tell you, the 1960s was a decade marked by incredible social upheaval: Civil Rights struggles, pro- and anti-Viet Nam War demonstrations, inner-city riots, the Women's Liberation movement, three assassinations (President John F. Kennedy, Dr. Martin Luther King Jr., and Senator Robert F. Kennedy), the Cuban Missile Crisis, Hippies, Woodstock, "free love," drug culture, the first moonwalk, etc. It was a tumultuous time.

And just as society in general was undergoing tremendous change, so was the world of the local service airlines. It was the decade when they really began to feel their oats, so much so that one *Aviation Week* writer would wax enthusiastic about their "evolution into small trunk carriers." They had formed their own lobbying organization, the Association of Local Transport Airlines (ALTA), and in 1966 ALTA produced "Jet Age Route Policy for Local Service Airlines, a report spelling out in detail how these airlines had grown in the ten years between 1955 and 1965.

As noted in the previous chapter, the combined fleet was larger, and a bit more up-to-date. In 1955 the total local fleet had numbered 169 aircraft, 93-percent of which were DC-3s. There were as yet no turboprops. Ten years later the picture had changed dramatically. Not only had the fleet more than doubled in size, it was much more diverse, with twin-engine Martin-Liners and Convair-Liners plus 56 turboprops. There were even two pure-jets (Mohawk's recently-acquired BAC 1-11s). Incredibly, there were still DC-3s, although 34 fewer than ten years earlier. Now the 123 DC-3s comprised approximately one-third of the total fleet.

To put all this into another perspective, in 1955 the locals' combined fleet offered a total of just 4,248 seats. Ten years later that number would jump to 13,410 available seats. Of these: 8,080 were on piston Convairs or Martins; 2,240 on turboprops; 138 on jets (Mohawk's); and still 2,952 on the venerable DC-3s.

And they were beginning to fill more of those seats. As *American Aviation* reported in 1966, "The 13 U.S. local service airlines recorded another year of rapid growth in 1965 – a growth that the forecasters say will continue at a rate of 15% a year – and the prospects look bright for expansion into denser short-haul markets." The story went on to report that five of the locals – Allegheny, North Central, Ozark, Piedmont, and Mohawk – had each carried a million or more passengers. The last three of that group, plus Bonanza and Pacific, had broken through the seemingly impossible-to-crack 50-percent load factor. But, as usual, not all the picture was so rosy. The average load factor for all 13 was still just 47.3-percent, and although revenues were up to $225M they were still reporting operating deficits, with no local expected to show a profit from operations much before the end of the 60s.

Meanwhile the trunks were beginning to see their gamble on purejets beginning to pay off. As early as March, 1960 Aviation Week was reporting that the "Domestic trunkline business, sparked by rapidly growing public acceptance of turbojet and turboprop aircraft, appears headed for another record year....Gross revenues are expected to climb 16% to top the $2 billion mark for the first time."

Perhaps that old musical question, "How ya gonna keep 'em / down on the farm / once they've seen 'paree'?" explains the phenomenon. As Davies notes in *Airlines of the U.S. Since 1914*, "To the American traveling public, the term jet conveyed an image of progress and sophistication that transcended practical considerations of timesaving, noise or vibration. Every domestic airline tried desperately to replace its piston-engined fleets without delay" and "The passengers quickly adapted themselves to the new standards, accepted all the publicity for the jets at face value, and tended to make disparaging remarks about the old 'coffee grinders.'"

And that demand for up-to-date transportation extended even to the shorter trips. "The operators began to sense the pressure to extend such service to all their route systems," notes Davies, "including the shorter segments....(Passengers) did not understand nor did they care about the theory of short-haul aircraft economics which held that the high fuel consumption of jet engines could be offset only by high block speeds and high annual utilization, neither of which could be achieved on short stages."

As fully detailed in the previous chapter, one local president, West Coast's Nicholas (Nick) Bez, sensed the passenger appeal and other virtues of jet-age equipment, and signed on to add the Fokker (Fairchild) F-27 to his fleet. West Coast's F-27s began service on September 27, 1958, almost four months before Eastern Air Lines' Lockheed L-188 Electra would enter service. Within a year Piedmont, Bonanza, Pacific, and Ozark were also offering F-27 service.

Other locals were finding slightly less expensive ways to add kerosene power to their fleets. One was by modifying airplanes they already owned, like the Convairs.

Between 1955 and 1957 the Military Air Transport Service (MATS) had tested an Allison turboprop-powered Convair called the YC-131C. Based on that success, Allison contracted with PacAero Engineering of Santa Monica to begin upgrading both Convair 340s and 440s with Allison 501D powerplants turning four-bladed constant-speed propellers. The combination became the long-lived Convair 580, which made its first proving flight on January 19, 1960.

Four-and-one-half years later, on July 1, 1964, Frontier launched Convair 580 service, the first airline to do so. The powerful airplane, which cruised almost 60 m.p.h. faster than a Convair 340, so impressed management that by the end of 1966 Frontier had converted all of its Convairs, at a cost of $500,000 to $650,000 per aircraft. Converting proved to be a wise move, for the turboprops were almost 20-percent less expensive to operate. Cost per aircraft-mile on a 100-mile stage length was approximately $1.22 for the Convair 340/440 while just .98 cents for the Convair 580.

Meanwhile, Convair had been developing its own conversion program using Rolls-Royce Dart powerplants. The modified Convair 240, called the Convair 600, made its first test flight on May 20, 1965 and entered service for Central on November 30, 1965. By 1968 all Convair 240s in the locals' fleets would be converted to Convair 600s. Central sent one of its Dart-powered Convairs on a publicity tour, making sure at every stop to position a dartboard, with a dart at the very center of the bulls-eye, next to the airplane as a photo-op for the local newspaper.

Honors for operating the shortest-lived conversion go to Allegheny for its Convair 540. In 1954 British engine manufacturer D. Napier and Sons proposed adding their Eland N.E1.1 turboprop engine to a Convair 340 – creating the Eland Convair 540, which had its first test flight February 9, 1955. Allegheny ordered six of these in a 52seat configuration and on July 1, 1959 began operating them on its unique Penn Commuter service – a space-available shuttle between Philadelphia and Pittsburgh, 260 miles apart. But in early 1962 Napier was absorbed by Rolls-Royce, ending production of and support for the Eland turboprop. Allegheny had the 540s re-converted to piston power.

Lake Central also earns honors for being sole operator of a little-known turboprop, although management probably came to regret that decision. The airplane, which some saw as the elusive DC-3 replacement, was the 27-seat Nord (now Aerospatiale) 262, powered by two Turbomeca Bastan VI turboprops. It first flew on December 24, 1962. Lake Central ordered eight of the Nord 262A and began service with them on October 31, 1965. Maybe Halloween is not the best day for an inaugural flight, because the Nords proved really scary. Ten months later on August 12, 1966, after two inflight engine failures and other incidents, the Nords were grounded for five months. It would be 1967 before they would fly again, although Lake Central was about to be absorbed by Allegheny. In 1974 Allegheny gave subsidiary Mohawk Air Services the task of upgrading the Nords with air conditioning, improved wing tips, and, most importantly, new engines. Fitted with reliable Pratt & Whitney of Canada PT6A-45s, the nine airplanes became Mohawk 298s, re-entering service in the first quarter of 1977.

Another one-of-a-kind local service turboprop, but a much more reliable one, was a Japanese-built 60-seat airliner chosen by Piedmont to eventually replace its Martin 4-0-4s. The airplane, which was the first post-war airliner to be built in Japan, was the Dart-powered

NAMC (Nihon Airplane Manufacturing Company) YS-11A. Created in July, 1959 NAMC was a consortium of six Japanese companies, including the well-known Fuji, Kawasaki, and Mitsubishi, charged with creating a short- to medium-range airliner for Japan's airlines. The YS-11's first flight was August 30, 1962. Less than six years later, on May 19, 1968, a YS-11A registered N156P would make the type's first flight in Piedmont colors, from Winston-Salem to Washington, D.C. It was *Blue Ridge Pacemaker* that day, but later would be re-named *Cherry Blossom Pacemaker*. Eventually Piedmont would own 21 of the type, mostly of the enhanced MTOW Series 500. On February 15, 1970 Piedmont retired its last Martin 4-0-4, making its fleet totally turbine. Piedmont's president Tom Davis praised the YS-11's ability to operate in and out of mountain airports as well as its maintenance reliability, which he called about the highest in the fleet. The YS-11s would remain with Piedmont until 1982.

Another fondly-remembered turboprop was the Fairchild-Hiller FH-227, a larger and stronger 52-seat version of the license-built Fairchild F-27. The handsome high-winged airplane made its inaugural test flight on January 27, 1966^2 and Mohawk began operating them on July 1, 1966 followed by Ozark in December and Piedmont in early 1967.

But what about "real" jets? In the first-half of the1960s pure-jet service to the smaller cities was still rare, even for the trunks. The Boeing 727-100 had its first revenue service on February 1, 1964, the BAC One-Eleven on April 25, 1965, the DC-9-10 on December 8, 1965, and the Boeing 737-200 on April 29, 1968. But these were all operated by trunk airlines; it would take a gutsy risk-taker like Mohawk's Bob Peach to once again lead the way for the locals. Later he would describe his airline's need for a larger airplane than the Convair 440 *Metropolitan*. When no U.S. manufacturer seemed interested at the time, he looked elsewhere, finding the BAC *1-11* (or One-Eleven), of which he said, "(this airplane) will continue Mohawk on a comparable basis with trunk airlines....Not only will air speed be increased, but ground time will be sharply reduced by a completely self-supporting, simplified ground-support system, including air-conditioning, heating, and starting equipment."

The search had begun in the summer of 1961 when Peach traveled to Europe to investigate two new short-haul jets, the British

Aircraft *Corporation's BAC One-Eleven* and Sud Aviation's *Caravelle*. On October 27, 1961, Mohawk's board agreed with Peach that the airline should provide jet service by the spring of 1965. It authorized him to negotiate with the British Aircraft Corporation for four jets and agreed to a $100,000 payment to the company upon signing a letter of intent."

The BAC product seemed ideal for Mohawk's needs. It could carry 69 passengers at 550 mph and operate out of most of the smaller airports on route system. As Peach wrote in his "Four-Seaters to Fan Jets" speech, "For the first time, the One-Eleven will provide Mohawk with an aircraft designed from the start with high-density, short-haul routes in mind."

He didn't realize it, but he was about to embark on a skirmish with Washington bureaucrats. In February of 1962 then- C.A.B. Chairman Alan S. Boyd assured Peach that the intended purchase made sense and actually seemed the only reasonable course for the airline. Thinking he had C.A.B. blessing, Peach signed an agreement with BAC on July 24, 1962, to purchase four One-Elevens for a total of $17M. That total was $2M more than MOH's assets, but management intended to finance by issuing $6M of convertible debentures bank loans, and internal financing.

But the C.A.B. staff was skeptical, doubting that jets were a good fit for the airline. The jet's 69 seats, 50% more than on the a Convair, meant that Mohawk would somehow have to increase its average 45- to 48-percent load factor to as high as 51-percent just to break even. Some in the C.A.B. objected to the use of taxpayer money being spent on a foreign-built airplane. Others were concerned that Mohawk would be "setting a dangerous precedent" luring other locals, with shakier financing, to add jets. As we'll see below, their fears were perfectly justified.

C.A.B. middle management several times tried to quash the deal, asking Mohawk to produce a forecast for system operations through 1966. But the airline was under no obligation to do so and Peach feared that such information could be used by American. Then, in mid-December of 1962, these staffers leaked a letter that Boyd had written Peach in which he warned against Mohawk's planned purchase. Both Peach and Sir George Edwards, Managing Director of BAC, protested to Boyd who said he was "surprised and chagrined" to learn that his letter had been made public. Peach, noting that "This business is never dull," would later reassure his Board that the airline would survive this skirmish with the C.A.B.

And survive it did, persevering to operate 24 *One-Eleven*s, including three acquired from Aloha and another three leased from Braniff, which had been the first domestic U.S. airline to acquire the type. Mohawk was a true pioneer, the first local to offer pure-jets, and a year ahead of all the other locals. Mohawk's *1-11* entered service in Mohawk's 20th Anniversary Year, on July 15, 1965, which was a little less than three months after Braniff's first *One-Eleven* began revenue service. Prior to the start of service Mohawk had put its new jet on display at an open house at Griffiss AFB in Rome, NY, and thousands came out to see the little twin-jet, which must have seemed relatively tiny compared to the USAF B-52s and KC-135s that called Griffiss home. By the end of March, 1966 the airline's five One-Elevens were becoming a hit with passengers, resulting in a 27-precent increase in emplanements and giving the lie to the C.A.B.'s earlier concerns. The airplane operated 14 segments per day and was capable of a ten-minute turn-around, making it just as much of a hit with Mohawk management.

But not with American Airlines' management, which began to grow concerned at Mohawk's business passengers' eager acceptance of the little twin-jet on runs from upstate cities to New York's LaGuardia. American had been a year behind Mohawk in the order book, and its *One-Eleven*s didn't begin arriving until nine months after Mohawk's first jet service. American promptly assigned them to the same routes as little Mohawk's. As Davies notes, for a Big Four airline to have to compete with and match the equipment of a local was a situation that the C.A.B., even in its wildest imaginings, could never have foreseen back in 1944.

Mohawk earned its place in the history books as the first local to operate a pure-jet and the only local to operate the *One-Eleven*. But it just barely retained the latter honor. Just as some in the C.A.B. had feared, in October, 1962 little Bonanza was now seeking permission to also purchase jets. In February, 1963 the C.A.B. denied the request, explaining that such a venture was sure to increase the airline's subsidy need.

But the lure of jet-power was growing. Douglas announced that it, too, had a 300- to 500-mile range airliner under consideration, and sent its sales teams off to introduce Model 2086, or its "Compact Jet" to the airlines. By April, 1962 Douglas had an actual mock-up to show, an estimated sales price of $3 million, a name – the DC-9, and a target delivery date of late 1964. What it needed, it said, were firm orders, at least 125 of them, before it could commit to production.

A year later Donald Douglas, Sr. announced that production had begun because careful research had convinced the company that there was a market for the new airplane. Historians note that, as it had with its DC-8, Douglas was taking a calculated risk; except for Delta Air Lines, none of the trunks had expressed any real interest, and would not for another year.

The Douglas DC-9-10 was available by April 1964, a year before the Mohawk jets would even start service. Although the DC-9 differed only slightly from the BAC product, the Douglas name still worked magic. The trunks led the way in the order book but the locals soon followed. As Davies notes in Airlines of the U.S., once again Douglas had come through with a reliable short-haul airliner. West Coast agreed. That airline, launch customer for the Fairchild F-27, announced, only a week after the DC-9's February 25, 1965 initial test flight, that its Board of Directors had authorized the purchase of three Douglas DC-9-10s for delivery in the summer of 1966. Writing in Air West, the in-house publication, Nick Bez, Jr. explained that they had evaluated several other possibilities but decided on the DC-9 because it seemed made for the small airline. He noted that the airplane could carry 70 passengers from a 5,000-foot runway and featured a self-contained stairway and a baggage door only 42 inches off the ramp – making it ideal for his airline's purposes

The early Boeing 737 might also have been ideal – had it been available. But the 737-100 wouldn't make its initial flight until April 9, 1967, and the 737-200 not until August 8, 1967, almost a full year after West Coast's first DC-9 revenue service, on September 26, 1966. Also frustrated by the delay was Pacific Airlines, which on September 13, 1965 ordered four Boeing 737s with options for four more. But since delivery would not be until 1968, the airline leased, with an option to buy, two Boeing 727-100s.

This gave Pacific a strange 'double first' honor – first local to <u>order</u> the 737 and first local to <u>operate</u> the 727. But it was not the first local to <u>order</u> the three-holer. That honor went to Frontier, which signed on for five 727-100s on August 11, 1965. Frontier began 727 service on September 30, 1966 and a year later ordered five 727-200s and five 737-200s. In 1969 it replaced its five original 727-100s with 737200s, a type upon which the airline would eventually standardize.

Of course, to the average passenger, a 'jet' was a 'jet,' and the differences between a 727, a 737, a DC-9, or a BAC 1-11 meant little. Realizing this, the airlines' marketing departments ignored technical specifications and set about to market the more colorful aspects of their new airplanes. For example, Bonanza began imaginatively promoting its two brand-new Douglas DC-9s as "FunJets".

The airline had ordered early, as far back as July, 1963, and even though the needed C.A.B. approval didn't come until March, 1964 the local had secured for itself a privileged position in the delivery queue, becoming, on December 19, 1965, second (after launch customer Delta) to take delivery of the newest Douglas product, a DC-9-11 (N945L). Management decided to delay the start of service until the second airplane, a DC-9-14 (N946L) was delivered on January 17, 1966. Finally on March 1, 1966 Bonanza began DC-9 service on three routes, including the lucrative and busy Los Angeles – Las Vegas run.

Bonanza needed jets in that market. Its turboprop Fairchild F-27s had been no match for Western's Boeing 720Bs, and Bonanza's revenue on that route had dropped by almost two-thirds, especially with Western charging only $13 for the 235-mile trip. So it created a full-color promotional brochure, *Take off thru the Land of Fun on Bonanza DC-9 Fun Jets*. The idea was to make the DC-9 more than just another airplane, and the brochure said passengers would be seated like "royalty in a contoured chair, serene in a luxurious lounge-like atmosphere – with a view of the world….through large 'picture' windows that always remain clear…that are sized and spaced to present all the grandeur of the upperworld for your personal approval."

All that might have appealed to vacationers seeking the sybaritic attractions of Las Vegas or Reno. But back in the heartland, Ozark's marketing department clearly understood the mid-westerner's respect for deferred gratification and hard work. In 1968 Ozark chose as its advertising symbol the " Go-Getter Bird," a cheerfully hyperactive cartoon bird in Ozark uniform, intended to appeal to the " Go-Getter," the ever-busy business traveler. The slogan became "Go-Getters Go

Ozark," and the advertising featured a " Go-Getter of the Year," played by George Carlin, the off-beat comedian.

Ozark's flight attendants, busier than any Go-Getter, probably would have welcomed some comic relief. The St. Louis – Dallas DC9 trip, which lasted only 90 minutes, featured "Wine Cellar Service," a kind of in-flight wine-tasting with three different wines plus cheese and finger sandwiches – served to 100 pax by three very fast-moving stewardesses. Then there were the Flair Meals, based on meals served by international airlines, served on the hour-long flight to Minneapolis. Understandably, the cabin crew hated those trips – but passengers loved them. Years later, after TWA had acquired Ozark, one TWA passenger, learning that his particular cabin crew was ex- Ozark, gushed, "Oh, I remember those little wicker baskets with the sandwiches and the wines."

Equally memorable were North Central's plastic packets filled with timetables, gift catalogues, brochures, and stickers featuring " Herman" – North Central's stylized mallard duck logo – that the airline gave to passengers on its DC-9s. And those passengers were flying to or from places like Green Bay, Wisconsin (227,000 pop.) or Rapid City, South Dakota (89,000) – places that were enjoying their first-ever jet service courtesy of North Central's DC-9s. And that phenomenon wasn't restricted to North Central. Just as they had once brought 'the little places' their first scheduled air service, the locals were now serving some of those same places with the same sort of equipment used by the trunk carriers.

Of course, having jets in their fleets didn't automatically erase all of the locals' problems, but the jets did work wonders in the image department. Or, as Bonanza's executive vice-president told *AvWeek* when Bonanza's DC-9 FunJets went into service, "We got past the hand-me-down image when the F-27s replaced the DC-3s, but that was just an interim step. Now, overnight we have leaped forward several years with equipment that equates with the best any carrier can offer."

Obviously, it was not so easy to ridicule your local airline when it was operating equipment identical to that of the trunks and when its timetables showed an increasing number of non-stops that actually competed head-to-head with the "big" airline. But that's a story best told in Chapter 8, "Business Class." In the meantime, let's look at some neat photos.

Chapter 6: Window Seat

Although by no means a photographic history of the Locals (it would take a much, much bigger book to do that task justice), the 14 following photos do broadly trace the growth of these airlines from second-level operators of second-hand equipment to players able to compete with the majors using newly-purchased aircraft indistinguishable, to the layman, from those operated by the larger and older airlines. To offer larger photos per page, the captions are found not below each photo but here. Numbers below correspond to the numbered photo in the pages following these captions.

#1: Pioneer Martin 2-0-2, " *Pacemaster* Kit Carson," airport unknown. Unfortunately, the C.A.B. objected vehemently to Pioneer's acquisition of the Martin 2-0-2s, and the resulting financial bind weakened the airline and left it vulnerable to Continental's later takeover bid. Full details are available in Chapter 4: "A Change of Planes."

#2: Southwest (later Pacific) DC-3, airport unknown. Of course this Southwest had zero relation to the famed Texas-based low-cost carrier of today. Southwest renamed itself Pacific Air Lines in March, 1958 and proudly served such little-known places as Coalinga, in central California.

#3: Bonanza DC-3, very likely a publicity photo. Bonanza would have been proud of its 'modern' airliner, as it had begun life as a charter operator with one four-seat Cessna 195, and before its 1949 certification as a Local it ran its first two DC-3s back and forth between Reno and Las Vegas, as an intrastate carrier.

#4: Mohawk Convair CV-240, "Air Chief Seneca," at what was then, in November, 1955, just "Newark Airport ("Liberty" was added post 9/11). This particular airplane was one of Mohawk's first three Convairs, acquired by way of China (details in Chapter 4: "A Change of Planes"). That helicopter visible just above mid-fuselage could be one of the Sikorsky S-55s that Mohawk briefly operated in 1955, the only Local to ever operate a helicopter service.

#5: Southern Martin 4-0-4 at Atlanta Municipal Airport (ATL), as that field was called until 1971. A sister ship, N144S, earned the honor of operating the very last piston-engine passenger flight by a certificated (non-commuter) US airline, on April 30, 1978.

#6: A *'Friendship* at Friendship.' An Allegheny F-27 *Friendship,* which the airline called a "VistaLiner," at Baltimore on December 22, 1966, when that airport was still known as Friendship International. It became Baltimore-Washington International (BWI) in 1973, and Baltimore/ Washington International Thurgood Marshall Airport in 2005. Allegheny was actually a late-adopter of the high-wing turboprop, with West Coast leading the way, then Piedmont, Bonanza, Pacific, and Ozark (see Chapter 4: "A Change of Planes").

#7: Piedmont NAMC YS-11A, also at Baltimore, on July 22, 1971. Piedmont's President Tom Davis extolled the type's reliability and its short-field capabilities, and they remained part of the Piedmont fleet until 1982 (see Chapter 5: "Jet-Propelled").

#8: Lake Central Nord (Aerospatiale) 262A at Baltimore on April 9, 1968, less than three months before that airline would become part of Allegheny. The Nord's engines had a reputation for severe maintenance problems, and several in-flight shut-downs caused the type to actually be grounded for five months (see Chapter 5: "Jet-Propelled").

#9: Central Convair CV-600 at Dallas-Love Airport on July 8, 1967, two months before Central would be absorbed into Frontier. Central was so proud of these Dart-powered Convair turboprops, in their sophisticated new livery, that it undertook a huge promotional campaign prominently displaying a dartboard with one centrally-placed dart at each stop.

#10: Trans-Texas DC-9 " Pamper Jet" at an unidentified airport, no date. The $50 million price tag for TTa's six DC-9s was a blow to the airline's pocketbook and one of the reasons for its financial death spiral that opened the door to its 1972 takeover by Frank Lorenzo (see Chapter 10: "Off the Radar Scope").

#11: Pacific 727 at San Francisco International (SFO) on May 5, 1967. Technically the airplane was now part of Air West, the new regional created by the three-way merger of Bonanza, Pacific, and West Coast on April 17, 1967. To Pacific goes the honor of first Local to operate the 727 (see Chapter 5: "Jet-Propelled").

#12: Frontier 737-200 at Denver-Stapleton (DEN) on August 27, 1972, at the beginning of a ten-year period of prosperity which saw the airline adding more jets and increasing its longer stage-length routes, especially after passage of the Airline Deregulation Act of 1978. The first Frontier 737s arrived in 1969, replacing the airline's 727-100s (see Chapter 5: "Jet-Propelled").

#13: Allegheny Commuter Shorts 360 at Philadelphia International (PHL), undated photo. The Allegheny Commuter brand dates to November 15, 1967, and by the end of 1974 a dozen smaller airlines had re-painted their airplanes with the Allegheny Commuter livery. The Locals, originally called "Feeders," now had their own 'feeders' (see Chapter 9: "A Slight Course Deviation").

#14: Air New England de Havilland DHC-6 *Twin Otter* at Arizona's Pinal Airpark (MZJ), a desert boneyard, in November, 1981, after the short-lived Local's October 31, 1981 cessation of operations (see Chapter 10: "Off the Radar Scope") The last Local to receive C.A.B. certification (January 20, 1975), Air New England's broad diagonal bands of vermilion, orange, olive, and blue easily could have won the 'Most Colorful Paint Scheme' award, had one existed.

Photographer: unknown; Photo courtesy John Wegg and *Airways* magazine.

Photographer: A. R. Krieger; Photo courtesy John Wegg and *Airways* magazine.

Photographer unknown; Photo courtesy John Wegg and *Airways* magazine.

Photographer Howard M. Svendsen; Photo courtesy John Wegg and *Airways magazine*.

Photographer Jay L. Sherlock; Photo courtesy John Wegg and *Airways* magazine.

Photographer David W. Lucabaugh; Photo courtesy John Wegg and *Airways* magazine.

Photographer David W. Lucabaugh; Photo courtesy John Wegg and *Airways* magazine.

Photographer David W. Lucabaugh; Photo courtesy John Wegg and *Airways* magazine.

Photographer: unknown; Photo courtesy John Wegg and *Airways* magazine.

Photographer: Howard M. Svendsen; Photo courtesy John Wegg and *Airways magazine*.

Photographer: Jay L. Sherlock; Photo courtesy John Wegg and *Airways* magazine.

Photographer: Jay L. Sherlock; Photo courtesy John Wegg and *Airways* magazine.

Photographer: Bob Redden; Photo courtesy John Wegg and *Airways magazine.*

Photographer: John Wegg; Photo courtesy John Wegg and Airways magazine.

Chapter 7: In-Flight Entertainment

*U*nfortunately, not much in the airline industry these days can be classified as 'fun,' with passengers both angry and demanding, employees overworked and worried about job security, and even executives concerned about their airline's prospects. But it wasn't always thus, as any veteran airline person could tell you. Especially anyone who worked for one of the local service airlines. "We were like family" and "We had fun" were two of the most common reactions from ex-local service employees interviewed for this book. Their airlines may have been "second level," and their equipment often second-hand, but they had a definite mission – to bring air service to a specific region – and, as a result, a spirit of camaraderie ---- or perhaps it was shared misery! Either way, they loved doing their jobs.

This chapter attempts to capture some of the lore of that long-gone time and relate some anecdotes which will help readers better appreciate those unique little airlines. So come back with us, to those good old days, so different from today. First we offer some Fascinating Factoids about the Locals, and then we present stories from each local, alphabetically.

Ten Local Firsts : Despite their early reputation as somehow a 'second level' of airline, the Locals actually achieved many significant innovations, or 'Firsts.' See if you can answer these ten questions, whose answers appear below.

1. First U.S. airline to operate the Fairchild F-27 turboprop was …?
2. First mainland U.S. airline to operate the NAMC YS-11A turboprop was …?
3. First U.S. airline to operate the Convair 600 turboprop was …?
4. First U.S. airline to operate the Nord 262 turboprop was …?
5. First U.S. airline to order the Convair 580 turboprop conversion was …?
6. First U.S. airline to operate the DC-9-51 was …?
7. First airline to order the Boeing 737-400 was …?
8. First all-female flight deck and cabin crew was aboard …?
9. First scheduled U.S. airline to hire an African-American "stewardess" was …?
10. First scheduled U.S. airline to hire a female pilot was …?

Answers: 1. West Coast; 2. Piedmont; 3. Central; 4. Lake Central; 5. Lake Central/ Frontier (Lake Central dropped its options, allowing Frontier the honor); 6. Allegheny; 7. Piedmont; 8. a Piedmont 737-200, May 10, 1982; 9. Mohawk; 10. Frontier.)

And a 'Last': To Southern Airways goes the credit of operating the very last piston-engine passenger flight by a certificated (noncommuter) US airline. On April 30, 1978 Southern's ship N144S, a Martin 404, operated Flight 753 (Atlanta - Gadsden, Alabama – Atlanta), earning itself a place in history before being sold.

One More Factoid: Of all the 13 locals permanently certificated in 1955, only Bonanza and West Coast never operated either a Convair or a Martin product, but moved directly from the DC-3 to the Fairchild F-27 and then to DC-9s.

The Opposite of Non-Stop: In their early days the locals were mandated to stop at every community named on the route certificate, making the route a series of 'hops' and confirming the general public's suspicion that these were indeed "puddle-jumpers." A Southern pilot recollected a trip from Tuscaloosa, Alabama to Columbus, Mississippi, some 53 miles away. In those days, cockpit doors could remain unlocked. A passenger, seated near the front row, yelled in, "Hey, Captain! Don't we fly over any towns?" Since they had just passed over Gordo, Alabama, this captain turned around and said, "Yes Sir, we just flew over one." And the smart-aleck passenger replied, "Hell, I mean without landing!"

Dissed : Although the locals' marketing departments worked hard to build a 'solid-and-respectable' image for their struggling carriers, much of their effort was lost on those 'other locals' – the very same people whom these airlines served. They had their own nicknames for 'their' airlines that served their areas: Allegheny was called "Agony,"; Mohawk was, of course, "Slohawk"; Ozark backwards was "Krazo"; Piedmont was "Peatmoss"; Trans-Texas was either "Tree-top" or "Tinker Toy"; and West Coast was often labeled "Wet Toast." It probably seemed funny to all but the particular airline's personnel.

Coulda Been A Contender – Part I: The locals will be forever associated with DC-3s, Convairs, and Martins. But there was another airplane that might have made the cut. The Beech *Model 34 Twin-Quad*, conceived as a 20-seater with a 1,400-mile range and a cruise speed of 180 mph, was designed specifically for what Beech management saw as a promising new market – the feeder airlines.

As described in Edward H. Phillips' *Beechcraft: Pursuit of Perfection*, the airplane had several unconventional design features, including:

(1) a V-tail similar to that on the Model 35 Beech *Bonanza*; (2) four engines driving just two props –in each wing were two 400 hp. 8cylinder Lycoming GSO-580 supercharged engines linked to the prop by a common gearbox; and (3) retractable tricycle-gear, a very modern touch.

The *Twin-Quad's* inaugural flight was October 1, 1947. On January 17, 1949, the prototype was badly damaged in a forced landing shortly after takeoff. With no orders from any of the fledgling feeder lines, Beech decided against repairing the damage and wrote the Twin-Quad off to experience.

Coulda Been A Contender – Part II : At their peak, the locals prided themselves on operating the same types of twin-jets – DC-9s and 737s – as their larger brethren. But they missed the chance to stand out, at least with airplane buffs, by operating a unique type.

That would have been the de Havilland D.H. 126 Small Turbofan Branchliner. At 60 feet 3 inches in length and with a 62-foot wingspan, it was actually smaller than the DC-3 (64'6" long, 95' wingspan) that it was intended to replace. According to the de Havilland company's brochure, the D.H. 126 would meet the needs of the locals for "an aircraft carrying about 30 passengers, or a mixed payload of about 6,500 lb. of passengers and freight, with low operating costs to operate over short stage lengths, in the main below 200 n.m., from airfield used by the DC-3 but to current standards of airworthiness."*

The D.H. 126 was to offer a choice of either the Rolls-Royce R.B. 172-3 turbofan or the de Havilland PS-92 turbofan. The 4,000 pounds of thrust and a 23,600 pound Maximum Take Off Weight was expected to produce a take-off distance of just 2,200 feet and a cruise speed of 405 mph (350 kts.) at 25,000-foot altitude. Double-slotted flaps were to give it a 3,300-foot landing distance and a stall speed of just 67 knots. The cabin was to offer 2 x 2 seating and a lav, although headroom in the aisle was just 6'3".

de Havilland began designing the D.H. 126, which in many ways resembled the BAC *One-Eleven*, in 1961 and expected the first production models to be available in 1965. But a lack of orders relegated it to "almost-ran" status, much as the Beech Model 34 (above).

* The de Havilland Aircraft Company, Ltd., *de Havilland 126 Small Turbofan Branchliner*, 1961: Hertfordshire, England, p. 7, courtesy de Havilland Aircraft Heritage Centre.

Allegheny

Ralph Nader vs. Allegheny: On an April day in 1972 consumer advocate, environmentalist, and future U.S. presidential candidate Ralph Nader headed off to a speaking engagement in Hartford, Connecticut. But the Allegheny flight was badly oversold, and the agent had to deny boarding to some passengers. Unfortunately for Mr. Nader, and then for the airline, he was one of those "bumped." He went off and filed a $100,000 to $150,000 lawsuit for punitive damages, claiming that he had missed an important fund-raising speech. And he won – sort of. A federal court later awarded him $25,010: the $25,000 in damages was a fraction of the amount for which he had sued, and $10 for the actual cost of his ticket.

French Girls: Some employees called it the "wine-and-cheese" treatment. Obviously it was definitely not your typical airline paint scheme. But from November 1968 until 1978, Allegheny operated nine ex- Lake Central Nord 262 twin-engine turboprops painted deep-purple-with-gold-trim. Together with Convair 580s, twelve of these airplanes had been acquired when Allegheny absorbed Lake Central in March 1968. Allegheny decided that, because they were French-built, each should have a French-sounding feminine name, ending with 'd'Allegheny,' painted in gold script just below the vertical stabilizer, which itself bore a gold fleur-de-lis. Thus, in alphabetic order, these "d'Allegheny girls" were: Brigitte (N26211), Celeste (N26208), Claudette (N26202), Colette (N26212), Michele (N26209), Monique (N26213), Nicole (N26203), Yvette (N26207), and Yvonne (N26201). Their stewardesses wore French-themed outfits. It was a rather over-the-top treatment for an airplane chronically plagued by engine problems. In fact, Allegheny had the Turbomeca engines on many of the Nords replaced with Pratt & Whitney engines, and called the refurbished airplanes Mohawk 298s. Most were sold to various Allegheny Commuter operators.

Bonanza

Little White Lie: Bonanza was an early adopter, transitioning directly from DC-3s to brand-new turboprops and skipping entirely the used Convair / Martin phase. Unlike West Coast, which was the first local to operate the Fairchild F-27A but which kept some DC3s around for many years, Bonanza quickly sold off its last DC-3, in November 1960. It made much of the modernization, proclaiming itself, as of November 1, 1969, "First all jet-powered airline in America" on timetables and bumper stickers.

Proud Parents: In January, 1966 Bonanza decided to show-off its brand-new DC-9 "FunJet" before putting it into service in March. They set up a schedule of five successive weekends, beginning January 29, to hold Open House in Las Vegas, Los Angeles, Phoenix, Reno, and Salt Lake City. Like many a Sun Belt resident, the marketing types forgot that winter can bring snow, especially in high-elevation Salt Lake City. But the white stuff didn't stop the locals from coming out to the airport, and so Bonanza employees happily shoveled a path across the ramp to show off their gleaming airplane. When the traveling show reached Phoenix so many people came out that the access road to Phoenix-Sky Harbor was blocked by huge traffic jams and Bonanza President Ed Converse spent hours inflating balloons to be distributed.

Central

A Mighty Wind: Yes, the DC-3 was a trifle slow for the 1950s – especially in a headwind. One pilot recalls chugging along at about 80 knots groundspeed. They had been flying parallel to the Santa Fe railroad tracks. Glancing down he noticed a train, possibly the famed Super Chief, below. Then he noticed it pulling ahead. His solution? To move directly over the tracks so that the passengers couldn't see the train passing them.

Show and Tell: Like many locals, Central encouraged employees to build bonds with the community. One way was to give tours to local schoolchildren visiting the airport on a field trip. The idea backfired one day for a group of second-graders touring a recently-arrived DC 3. The stewardess showed them the cockpit and let them sit in the seats. Then, as they were trooping down the slanted aisle, she unwisely decided to show them the lav. Bad idea, because it was occupied – by the crusty old captain sitting on the commode. The rattled stewardess stammered "And this is our captain" and quickly slammed the door.

Frontier

Sight-seeing: Anyone who loves to watch the passing scene from seat 10A would have really appreciated this little touch of customer care provided by Frontier, even late in its history. The inflight magazine carried sight-seeing guides so passengers could use the seat-back route map to appreciate the passing scenery. One example described where to locate Lookout Mountain, site of Buffalo Bill's grave, and named the towns visible from the 15,000 foot altitude expected six minutes after departure from Denver. Another tip was to look for Mount Evans, home to the world's highest automobile road. It was a far cry from today's uninformative and unfelt "now sit back and enjoy your flight."

Nap-Time: A Frontier flight attendant swore this happened. On a Denver – Kansas City – St. Louis trip one of the passengers was a real Old-West "cowpoke" type who looked as if he had just come in from riding the range. Soon after takeoff he disappeared into the lav, carrying a little satchel. Ten minutes later he emerged, dressed in pajamas and slippers. He shuffled back to his seat, took the blanket and pillow from the open overhead rack, stood on his seat, and was attempting to climb into that overhead rack when the almost-speechless flight attendant managed to exclaim "Sir, what do you think you're doing?" His reply, "I'm just trying to get into this here bunk!" He later admitted it was his first-ever airplane trip, he figured it would take a while, and since he was tired he thought he'd catch some shut-eye.

Takes a Licking and Keeps on Ticking: Even though it was Easter Sunday, the 23 passengers aboard Frontier's Flight 7 that April 21, 1957 thought they were in for a routine 40 minute hop from Prescott to Phoenix, Arizona. They hadn't contemplated having a close encounter with a mountain. But as the DC-3, Frontier's N65276, lumbered along between the Bradshaw and New River mountain ranges, the VFR conditions were rapidly deteriorating. Faced with a rapidly lowering ceiling, the pilots informed Air Traffic Control that they would be requesting an IFR clearance once they reached Knob intersection. Then the airplane, caught in a strong downdraft, began losing altitude and settling into a low cloud bank. As the pilots struggled to maintain altitude there was a horrendous crunch and the airplane skidded crazily to the right. Fighting the controls, the pilots got the airplane stabilized and, once out of the downdraft, it began climbing. Breaking out of the clouds the panicked crew instinctively looked to their left, and discovered that the outer 12 feet of left wing were missing. But, with the airplane holding altitude and no alternate airport nearby, they continued on to Phoenix, landing just two minutes later than scheduled. Although the story is a tribute both to the pilots' skill and to the strength of the DC-3, other Frontier pilots were spooked by that particular aircraft, as it seemed to have a suicidal streak. It was responsible for Frontier's only fatal accident.

On December 21, operating as a freighter, it crashed and burned on takeoff from Denver, killing both pilots.

Wildly Windy West: Casper, Wyoming can be a very windy place, as some Frontier ramp workers learned one night when the stronger-than-usual wind started blowing golf bags off a belt loader. Then it snatched the "Kwickee" small air-freight bag from one ramp agent's grasp and sent it whooshing off into the night. The bag held the weekly payroll checks for the local oil company's workers, who were used to getting paid on a regular basis and not used to airline employees losing their paychecks. One 'rampie' suggested taking a similar bag, releasing it into the howling wind, and following it with a four-wheel drive truck, assuming it would lead them to its counterpart. No one took his idea seriously and eventually an airport worker discovered the original Kwickee bag caught in the perimeter fence. At Omaha one night it wasn't nature but a 737 that caused the wind. The Boeing was just departing its gate, but someone forgot to stop the passengers deplaning a Convair 580 at the next gate. The jet blast mischievously singled out passengers with toupees, who found themselves chasing their hair pieces across the ramp.

Lake Central

A Very Local Local: The airline was proud of its service to the region often called the heartland of America. In 1967 Lake Central re-did its livery, painting a large heart on the tails of its airplanes and calling itself "The Airline With a Heart." In the Fifties one of its advertisements read, "If it ends in 'burg,' 'ville', or 'town' we probably fly there. Often." And yet it was also aware of its role as a small but essential link to the world. Promotional material developed by the airline read, "…anyone in the area served by Lake Central is only 36 hours from anyplace in the world….whether you are in Kokomo…or Kalamzoo…."

Flying Streetcar?: The area served by Lake Central had once been served by a form of rail transportation called the "Interurban." Larger and faster than typical city streetcars, the interurbans were at their height in the first two decades of the 20th Century, carrying passengers between cities or from city to rural area. But as automobiles and highways became more common the interurbans declined in popularity. Yet, to regional residents with long memories, Lake Central, with its relatively short hops between heartland cities, reminded them of that earlier mode of travel – hence the Lake Central nickname: The Flying Interurban.

Mohawk

Injuns!: From 1951 until the mid-1960s Mohawk capitalized strongly on the Native American theme. The airline was "The Route of the Air Chiefs" and its DC-3s, Convairs, and all but two Martins had names beginning with "Air Chief," as in "Air Chief Algonquin" or "Air Chief Tecumseh." Its early logo was a stylized and silhouetted Native American face in a circle with "feathers" streaming backward. And then there was " Lil Moh" a grinning cartoonish "Indian brave" who appeared on company publications and in advertisements. Mohawk even went so far as to arrange for a real Native American, a lad from the Onondaga Reservation, to appear in native clothing at various photo ops as a "living trademark." In today's atmosphere of political correctness, such behavior would probably invite lawsuits. Of course, had fate gone differently, the whole issue could have been a moot point. The airline could just as easily have been named Atlantic or Yankee Airlines. Those were the second- and third-place winners when Robinson Airlines conducted an in-house competition for a new name. Some 2,000 employees voted, and the Board of Directors adopted the Mohawk name in 1951. Actually, with the arrival of the Fairchild Hiller FH-227 and the BAC One-Eleven, the "Air Chief" names disappeared. The turboprops were all named for cities on the route map, such as "City of Watertown" while the pure-jets were mostly named for states (although N1120J bore dual names: New Jersey/Robert E. Peach).

Mohawk's Fling Wing Fling: In the summer of 1954 Mohawk became the first and only local to operate scheduled helicopter service. The airport at Liberty-Monticello, in the heart of New York's Catskill Mountains, was inadequate for DC-3 service. So the airline acquired Sikorsky S-55s to ferry passengers from Newark Airport to the resort area famous for Grossinger's and other "Borscht-Belt" hotels. The airline boasted that the 82-mile trip was the longest scheduled nonstop helicopter flight operated in the U.S. The fare was $19.80 one-way ($159.29 in 2008 dollars), a bit pricey for a one-hour flight in a craft that vibrated like a washing machine. Mohawk dropped the service that Fall.

Never Say Goodbye: In September, 1960, Mohawk made good use of its aging DC-3s. It refitted the interiors with red velvet curtains and red brocade wallpaper. Outside there was a large yellow-and-black gas lamp on each bright red tail plus ornate gold pin-striping and the word's " Mohawk Gas Light Service" above the windows. The idea was to lure the male business traveler. To help these Alpha-male types forget that they were traveling at one-third to one-half the airspeed of a more modern airplane, there was free beer as well as free cheese and free pretzels. At the beginning the flights were labeled "Men Only," but eventually the airline relented and sold seats to both womenfolk and children, although these had to sit in the "Family Parlor" section safe from drinking, and possibly rowdy, men-folk. To keep with the Victorian-era theme, the flights were numbered 1890 through 1893.

North Central

Not Just Another Pretty Face: Like several other airlines, North Central originally used stewards (male cabin attendants) to tend to passenger needs. But, legend has it, North Central began hiring females in 1954 after famed newspaper columnist Westbrook Pegler described his trip with North Central. Everything was fine, he wrote, except for the fact that there was a 1900-pound "gorilla" taking care of the cabin rather than a pretty girl.

Duck!: North Central's logo, a stylized mallard in flight, was so well-loved that it even appeared on the airplanes of Republic, the airline formed by the merger of North Central and Southern. " Herman-the-duck" was once voted as one of the most widely recognized logos, up there with PanAm's globe.

Ozark

Poor Paintjob: In its rush to start service, Ozark had its DC-3s, obtained from Parks, repainted as quickly as possible. To save time, employees painted out the "P" and the "S" of "Parks" and painted an "OZ" in front of the ARK of the Parks name, But one employee left out the "Z" on one airplane, which flew for many months carrying the name, "OARK AIRLINES." Management decided to leave the misspelling and mismatched paint scheme intact to prove to customers that Ozark had more than one airplane. At that time they had four DC-3s and 40 employees.

Ol' Stinky: In 1972, to compete with commuter carrier Air Illinois, which had been offering service from the state capital directly to Chicago's former lakefront airport, Meigs Field, Ozark leased three de Havilland Canada DHC-6 Twin Otters from a Florida-based airline, Mackey International. Operating in Florida means almost year-round heat and humidity. Legend has it that the seats on these particular airplanes had become so sweat-soaked from years of passenger perspiration that, when the cabin temperature climbed, they exuded an aroma best-described as Arome du Gymnase (Gymnasium smell). In fact, some suggest that if Ozark's Fairchild FH-227s were known in-house as "Kerosene Queens" then the Twin Otters should have been called "Sweat Hogs." Ozark never made a profit on the Meigs flights and abandoned the service in 1974.

You Call This Sexy?!?: An Ozark DC-9-32 had a somewhat 'lurid' (at least by Midwest standards) past history. Registered N950PB, the airplane (msn47394/ln458) had once been Playboy founder Hugh Hefner's famed "Black Bunny." Ozark leased it from Purdue Airlines and operated it between October, 1972 and March, 1976

Don't Call Us, We'll Call You: Shortly after Ozark began service to New York City, it discovered that somehow it had missed the deadline to be included in the new telephone book. So it turned a would-be disaster around by advertising that it was "The Only Airline In New York With An Unlisted Number." Ironically, in 2007, XLCC (X-treme Low Cost Carrier) Skybus boasted that it had no phone number and wanted all reservations made via the Web. Unfortunately it succumbed to the 2008 fuel-price crisis.

With Our Compliments: In this era of price-sensitive travelers and airlines selling meals at $8.00 a pop, it is hard to believe that airlines once gave things away. But they did, and Ozark's offerings were among the best. For example, should female passengers be stranded someplace overnight the airline offered them "Remain Over Night" (RON) kits,

a seven-inch by three-inch plastic envelopes containing tiny white vials of "RON Hand Cream," "RON Cleansing Cream," and "RON Hair Spray." It also held a nail polish remover pad, a sewing kit, and, of course, a nail file, toothbrush, toothpaste, and shower cap. The airline also gave away six-inch plastic rulers bearing the Ozark three-swallows and the legend "Line yourself up with Ozark Air Lines." And for the kids there were put-together Styrofoam gliders carrying the Ozark logo or the 'Presto Magic Air Travel Game' featuring rub-on transfers for four scenarios: Airport, Big City, Snow Scene, and Beach.

Pacific

That's Not Exactly What We Meant: In 1966 Pacific asked employees for suggestions on how the company could best improve. One pilot wrote that the airline should "Create a dynamic, aggressive posture ... inspire a confidence in our airline ... and advertise it to the world." So much for listening to employees. The airline did advertise itself to the world, but in a memorable way. It hired the offbeat comedian/advertising man Stan Freberg to create what became known as the " Sweaty Palms" campaign, which launched on April 28, 1967 with a full-page ad in The New York Times. The headline screamed "Hey there! You with the sweat in your palms," and the copy claimed that "most people are scared witless" of flying. Even the pilots are sometimes apprehensive, the ad said, and so Pacific, instead of ignoring fear was planning to address it. The bulk of the campaign involved providing stewardesses with a Freberg-written script full of weak attempts at humor, such as having a stewardess hold up a blanket and announce "we will now demonstrate the appropriate use of the security blanket" A month later the airline began handing out "survival kits" with miniature security blankets and imitation rabbits feet. The campaign, which didn't exactly play well with the general public, was hated by the rest of the industry, which saw it as an act of desperation by a failing airline. By June, 1967 Pacific and West Coast were already talking merger. West Coast's blunt-spoken president Nick Bez told The Times that he didn't like the campaign. "It scared people away from the airline; we don't like to do those things," he said.

Piedmont

Flying Coffin: Piedmont's third DC-3 spooked passengers. The leased airplane had a "cargo compartment" made of two long wooden boxes placed near the door. Startled emplaning passengers at first thought they were coffins.

An Airplane With a Past: Piedmont was growing so quickly between 1977 and 1978 that it couldn't wait for deliveries and needed to add capacity a.s.a.p. It acquired six 727-100s, one of which, N838N or Mount Mitchell Pacemaker, was the famed, or infamous, airplane that "D. B. Cooper" had hijacked on November 24, 1971, when it belonged to Northwest Airlines.

You Sure This is a Long Range Airplane?: Piedmont started serving Los Angeles from its Charlotte, North Carolina hub with Boeing 727-200LRs acquired from Western and PSA. But these "Long Rangers" sometimes weren't. Whenever the winds aloft didn't cooperate the airplanes had to refuel at Denver. Passengers didn't always mind, however, because Piedmont gave each $20 whenever this happened.

You Made Us Famous: Once Piedmont began servicing NYC it needed to make its presence known. Television commercials were too expensive, but a clever advertising company with a New York City attitude came up with a catchy slogan whose double-entendre was designed to appeal even to jaded New Yorkers . Attached to the sides of taxicabs and buses, the billboard read "Piedmont Airlines Puts New York City on the Map."

Pioneer

A Faint Rattling Sound: Station managers, especially those at the smaller towns, prided themselves on being able to handle multiple jobs, including ticket counter agent, ramp agent, etc. And snake hunter. One of the towns Pioneer served was Clovis, New Mexico via Cannon Air Force Base. The farming/ranching town of Clovis (pop. 45,000) sits some 220 miles east of Albuquerque on eastern New Mexico's hot-and-dry high plains. Locals know this is rattlesnake country. So whenever a Pioneer flight arrived or departed the station manager had to go out with his shotgun and make sure the little wooden bridge over the gulley between the "terminal building" and ramp was clear of rattlers and other varmints.

Southern

That's Nice!: A cultural icon of the first half of the 1970s was "The Smiley Face," that yellow circle with two dots for eyes, an upward curving line for a mouth, and often the mindless entreaty to "Have a Nice Day!" Southern latched on to it big time. The yellow Smiley

Face adorned the radome of its DC-9s; above the yellow circle was the "Have a Nice Day" inscription and below was " Southern Airways." One publicity photo had four Southern flight attendants in 70's-era hot pants, black stockings, and go-go boots, "painting" the radome for the camera. And Southern really bought into the "Nice" theme. It ran an ad in Flight asking "How does the smallest regional airline get along with all of you bigger guys? Nicely, thank you. The ad showed a stylized Southern DC-9 carrying the yellow Smiley Face and the words Have a Nice Day on the radome. The ad ended with " Southern Airways: We serve the nicest people the nicest way we know."

The New South: Only a region secure with its past and positive of its future could risk telling jokes on itself, as Southern once did. Celebrating its new long-range routes, the airline ran an advertisement headlined "Sherman didn't by-pass Atlanta ... but you can" and urged travelers to "Jet direct" from New York's LaGuardia on "quick, quiet FanJETS" to Columbus, Georgia or Dothan, Alabama, bypassing the Atlanta connection. It takes guts to joke about the Union general, William Tecumseh Sherman, whose 1864 siege of Atlanta and subsequent march to the sea marked the beginning of the end of The Confederacy.

Southern Hospitality: Southern consciously practiced the "Hospitality... Southern Style" that its light blue soft-drink cups promised. An airline historian remembers: "Every passenger was treated with respect and given a warm welcome. On the DC-3s boxed lunches were handed out, and coffee, soft, and mixed drinks were provided. One former stewardess recalled how the old boxed lunches reminded her of Sunday "dinner on the grounds" at a Southern Baptist Church ...Once the airline received the Martinliners they began a modest in-flight service with hot meals. The Martins did not have fold-down trays on their seat backs so the stewardess laid a pillow across the passenger's lap and placed the hot food tray on the pillow. The Mint Julep became the official drink for in-flight services and steak, pot roast, and fried chicken became the mainstay of food service. The stewardesses were called Southern Belles and their uniforms included a broad hat (reminiscent of the antebellum period)."

Class Consciousness: One memorable television commercial depicted an emplaning passenger walking through what is obviously a bacchanalian version of First Class, with toga-clad women peeling grapes for ecstatic male passengers while the wine flows freely. The passenger then walks into Coach, where the other sweating pax are seated as if on an ancient Roman Galley while a stewardess menaces them with a whip. Then came the tagline: "No One is Second Class on Southern!"

Later, 'Gator!: Southern got more than it hoped for when it arranged a media event to mark its inauguration of DC-9 service to Chicago on April 1, 1970. President Frank Hulse showed up at Chicago Midway accompanied by "Susannah Southern," an actress wearing a pre-Civil War hoop skirt, and two alligators. Although alligators are common only to the deep south, someone thought it would be great idea to bring them along as symbolic of the mysteries of that part of the country. Animal experts had assured everyone that the reptiles would fall asleep during the flight and remain drowsy. But one alligator never bought into the agreement. It awoke and headed into the crowd, sending the members of a local high school band shrieking for their lives. A local fireman captured it and got it back into its cage, but the cameras were rolling and the incident earned top media coverage.

Texas International

Only Slightly Used: On September 30, 1966 TI took delivery of a "New/Used" DC-9-14. The airplane, actually Line Number 1 from the McDonnell-Douglas Long Beach assembly plant, already had 579 hours and 629 landings. Because of order backlogs TI would have had to wait two years to receive its first DC-9. But Douglas was able to sell the airline Ship One, which had been serving as a flying test bed up until April 30, 1966. Douglas then removed all the test equipment, configured it to a –14 standard, installed a 75-seat interior with TI fabrics, and re-registered it. N1301T. At the time of the Continental merger in 1982, Ship One had accumulated 56,070 landings in 42,365 flight hours – a very hard-working local service airplane. Continental sold it on May 13, 1983 but it soldiered on in various identities until July, 1992, when it finally became a spare parts trove. At that point it had 58,420 hours and 71,064 landings.

En Espagñol, Por Favor: Trans Texas' first five airplanes were all ex- American Airlines' DC-3s. Although political correctness was unheard of in 1947, someone thought it would be a good idea to paint the Spanish name for a species of bird just aft of each cockpit side window. The names chosen were: La Gansa (The Goose), La Aguila (The Eagle), La Paloma (The Dove), La Golondrina (The Swallow), or La Ciguena (The Stork). Unfortunately, whoever picked the names had an imperfect understanding of Spanish culture, in which eagles are generally understood to be masculine. Thus the name should have been "El Aguila." No one noticed, of course – except perhaps for the thousands of Spanish-speaking residents of the Lone Star State.

Boys and Their Toys: The very first group of Trans-Texas pilots were, as might be expected, WWII bomber pilots. They looked upon the comparatively "little" DC-3 as a relative toy, obviously a piece of cake to fly. Until the route-proving flight, one day before the start of revenue service. Onto old N336534, a.k.a. La Gansa, or The Goose, management packed 16 pilots, the Manger of Flight Ops, and a hapless young female office assistant to act as "stewardess." They set off on a familiarization run from Houston-Hobby to five other airports on TTa's route. The plan was for pairs of pilots, many of whom had never flown together previously, to demonstrate "correct" landing and takeoff procedures to their peers assembled in back. The peers, of course, were more interested in letting their inner teenager loose on the poor "stewardess" – until the Manager of Flight Ops ordered them to cease and desist. And that cockiness was soon to disappear. The DC-3 may be a forgiving airplane, but it can also embarrass the inexperienced. Each landing turned into a series of porpoising bounces and lurches, with catcalls and insults shouted from the unhappy "audience." Then there was the hot and high landing where the airplane ran out of runway and ground speed at approximately the same time – but with its tailwheel still high off the runway. Gravity took over and brought it down – hard. The group finally made it back to Houston, but an observer recalled that where 16 brash young hotshots had boarded that airplane in the morning, 16 very humbled men deplaned that night.

West Coast

The Barber of Seattle: West Coast's initial DC-9 revenue flight was on September 26, 1966. Among the invited guests was a barber. Some 20 years earlier he had worked at Boeing Field, although he lived 47 miles (76 km) away in the Washington State capital, Olympia. He was West Coast's first passenger, and claimed he had just been waiting for the day when he could fly between home and work. He had since retired and moved to California, but West Coast remembered, located him, and made sure he could attend the ceremony.

Don't Forget to Feed the Cargo: It's easy to forget that cargo made up a substantial revenue stream for the locals, especially in the early days. And sometimes that cargo had teeth – and big ones. One West Coast flight picked up a cage containing two fairly large lion cubs at Medford, Oregon. Later, at Corvallis, Oregon, agents loaded a crate of prize leghorn roosters, making sure to keep the two crates far apart.

At takeoff pilots thought they heard a commotion from baggage compartment. Their suspicions were confirmed when they landed at Portland. The well-meaning ramp agent unbuttoned the cargo hold only to come face to face with a snarling lion cub, its face full of chicken blood and feathers. He slammed the door shut and yelled for assistance. But as long as there were no predators on board most birds did survive, perhaps too well. Sometimes pigeon fanciers would ship a crate of homing pigeons, complete with instructions about how and when to release their darlings. Once a West Coast agent had to set his alarm for 0300, drive out to the field, and open the crate to start the pigeons off on their race.

Going Out In Style: West Coast's last DC-3 flight came June 30, 1968, one day before it, Bonanza, and Pacific would formally become Air West. The airplane (tail # N1051N) was the fifth DC-3 acquired by West Coast and saw 22 years of service. Painted in Air West colors, her final trip for West Coast was from Seattle to Portland to Astoria, Oregon, near the mouth of the Columbia River. It was billed as the "last DC-3 in scheduled airline service west of the Rockies" and the passengers all received certificates inducting them into "Loyal Order of Gooney Birds"

Rags to Riches: In 1960 West Coast's founder Nick Bez hosted a small party for himself at Seattle's exclusive Rainier Club. Actually it was not that small, as the guest list numbered 500 of the famous, wealthy, and powerful. Included were U.S. Senator Warren Magnuson, who was elected to the Senate in 1944, the same year that the C.A.B. created the locals, and Charles Willis, then-President of Alaska Airlines. The party invitations read "It would give me great pleasure if you would share with me the joy of toasting the 50th anniversary of my arrival in the United States." Bez had come to the U.S. as a 14-year-old immigrant from the Dalmatian coast of the former Yugoslavia and went on to make his fortune in the fish-packing business. He counted President Truman as one of his many personal friends.

These are just some of the many wonderful anecdotes from the four decades of the Locals' existence. If you worked for one of the Locals you probably have your own set of tales – and some might even be printable! It was a very different time, and we'll never see its like again.

Chapter 8: Business Class

Let's face it: no matter how much we aviation buffs like to discuss the latest equipment, route changes, color schemes, etc. we know at heart that the airline industry is, first and foremost, about business and economics. Sure, economics is not always the most exciting topic, but understanding certain aspects is essential – especially if one wants to understand the unique history of the Locals.

Although born of a federal mandate, these airlines were privately- or publicly-held entities whose goal it was to eventually become profitable for their owners or investors. But earning a profit was not always so easy for the Locals, for many reasons.

The major reason is that, in the beginning at least, the Locals were primarily short-haul operators, which is, if not a guaranteed money-loser, certainly only minimally profitable. Add to that the reality that the Locals originally served small towns with a low traffic potential. Even today, as a Government Accounting Office report noted, such smaller communities "typically lack the population base and level of economic activity that would generate sufficient passenger demand to make them profitable to air carriers." Of course, in today's deregulated environment, an airline (unless it is being subsidized under Essential Air Service rules) will quickly drop any place with low boarding numbers. But that was not the case under C.A.B. regulation.

As noted earlier, the C.A.B. was well aware that this new class of airline would require support, and it provided that support in many ways, from direct subsidy to route-strengthening to its "Use-It-OrLose-It" policy to allowing for some creative marketing promotions. This chapter will briefly examine these issues.

That Subsidy Thing:

Throughout their 40+ years of existence, the Locals always had 'the subsidy thing' attached to their image. Fiscal conservatives attacked subsidy as a waste of taxpayer dollars. Even President Kennedy, certainly no conservative, said there had to be a way to reduce what seemed to be spiraling federal subsidies.

Supporters of the Locals replied that subsidies supported <u>not</u> the airlines but the communities served, allowing them to have scheduled airline service. Another defense was to argue that the Locals actually returned money – sometimes as much as was being distributed – to the federal coffers because of the Federal transportation taxes collected.

Actually <u>both</u> sides forgot that subsidized air travel did <u>not</u> originate with the Locals. In 1938, before Local Service Airlines existed, the Civil Aeronautics Act authorized federal subsidy to the existing airlines, and by 1939 some 22 of these were receiving federal subsidy.

Actually the precedent for subsidy was the early airmail contracts, as federal payments often exceeded the actual cost of carrying the mail, thus creating an indirect subsidy. That continued until 1950 when, at the urging of then-President Harry S. Truman, there began a groundswell to separate airline subsidy from mail-pay. C.A.B. Chairman Donald W. Nyrop (later C.E.O. of Northwest Airlines) persuaded The Big Four (American, Eastern, TWA, and United) not only to accept reimbursement only for actual costs but also to return nearly $5 million in past overpayments. In the following 17 months another ten trunks would be placed on subsidy-free mail rates, saving the taxpayers an estimated $13 million annually.

While the trunks were able to operate without federal assistance, the Locals could not, as the C.A.B. expected of airlines mandated to serve 'thin' routes. For example, in 1950 Trans-Texas had extremely low load factors, with 60-percent of its 'city pairs' averaging less than one passenger <u>every three days</u>. But Trans-Texas provided the only airline service for 17 of its 26 destinations. Nor was TTA alone – for at one time nine of the Locals provided the only airline service to more than 50-percent of their cities. Two had even higher sole-provider percentages: Wisconsin Central (later North Central) was the only airline for 68.2-percent of its upper Midwest towns, and West Coast for 66.7-percent of its Pacific Northwest destinations.

Okay, argued the anti- subsidy types, we agree that subsidy might be necessary to guarantee service to these communities, but why does it keep climbing? And they would hammer away at the huge increases, such as the $43 million jump between 1954 and 1967 and at the fact that much of the money was going to create a more favorable rate of return for investors in those airlines.

But, countered the Locals' supporters, look at the big picture and see how subsidy <u>as a percent of total revenue</u> has consistently declined. In 1952, they said, subsidy accounted for almost 52% of the Locals' total revenue whereas by 1976 it was only four percent. And, where it had once been as high as $30.24 per passenger (in the very early year of 1947) it had dropped to just $1.82 by 1976. Of course these are skewed statistics since the Locals were carrying many more passengers and earning much more revenue in 1976 than 30 years earlier.

And thus the pro- and anti- subsidy forces did battle, year after year, even as C.A.B. policy changed, with the Board tightening the fiscal reins, going from a cost-plus policy to an attempt to have the Locals return a portion of their profits. There were a series of adjustments in class rates and, after 1966, profitable non-stop route awards were made subsidy-ineligible. Still the Locals complained that they were inadequately compensated and fiscal conservatives complained about Washington wasting money.

The argument was never really resolved and actually subsidy continues even now, as deregulation's Essential Air Service provision still provides for the subsidization of airline service to less-profitable smaller communities. And there are federal subsidies for other forms of public transportation, including Amtrak, the passenger railroad system which was once estimated to lose $1.70 for every $1.00 in revenue. Without massive infusions of federal and state dollars it would surely collapse, a fact realized by even the most fiscally conservative. That would include none other than President George W. Bush, who, as Governor of Texas in the late 1990s, approved a $5.6 million loan to keep Amtrak service at a handful of small Texas communities at the behest of a coalition of local mayors. That didn't seem so very odd to anyone familiar with the story of the Locals.

Fares:

Although the C.A.B. strictly controlled entry to and exit from markets, it played a milder oversight role with regard to fares, considering a fare rollback if it thought profits were excessive (rare, but possible) but approving fare increases to compensate for a drop in demand. That would seem counter-intuitive, but in those days air travel was not a market-based economy and the C.A.B. was committed to the airlines' health.

In 1956, at the urging of Congress, the Board established a general policy that said, in part, fares should reflect the costs of providing the service and that carriers were entitled to a reasonable ROI (Return on Investment) of 10.5-percent. That lasted until 1970 when a new investigation allowed the Locals to have a slightly larger ROI than the trunks although not as large as the Locals had wanted. That year also brought, over the protests of the trunks, the first joint fare arrangement between themselves and the Locals.

A few years later, the C.A.B. formally acknowledged what everyone already knew – that short-haul is more costly than long-haul – and took steps to make fares reflect this fact, increasing short-haul and reducing long-haul fares. It also said that the Locals should be allowed to charge as much as 130% over basic fares, subject to approval on a market-by-market basis. This would give the Locals more price flexibility to experiment – which meant they could try some creative promotional fares.

The Locals didn't create promotional fares (Capitol's 1948 Off-Peak Night Coach fare gets that honor), but they did get quite creative with them – seeking to attract price-sensitive leisure travelers while preventing their bread-and-butter, the business traveler, from using them. The trick was to market to subgroups:

◊ One such group was non-residents of the U.S. – ironic considering today's restrictions on non-citizens. But these were simpler times, and the Visit USA Unlimited Travel program was a draw. The program, which offered a 21-day $150 ($75 for those under 21) pass, was not limited to the Locals. Most trunk airlines participated. But for the Locals the program included an unusual spin. Besides requiring that participants reside "more than 100 miles outside of the border of any state in the U.S." it also mandated that if travel was to include <u>any</u> Local Service Airline, <u>it had to involve at least two</u>. The OAG, or Official Airline Guide (remember, this was pre-Web) provided a list of 65 cities where travelers could transfer <u>between Locals</u> – places like Minot, North Dakota where one could switch between Frontier and North Central.

◊ In addition to the industry-wide Visit USA promotion, several Locals set up their own promotions. Allegheny had "Vistaland,"
Bonanza had the eponymous "Bonanzaland," and, way out in California, Pacific had, "Wonderland." The latter two promotions were restricted to easterners.

◊ There were other, somewhat quirky, special fares such as Clergy Fares offering 50-percent discounted travel to "Ministers of Religion." In November, 1965 Trans-Texas offered "First Time Rider," a "$25.00 flat fare valid for 30 days" available to "anyone 21 years or over who had <u>never</u> flown on a certified air carrier before." A passenger had to present proof that this was indeed his initial flight experience, and the airline used its new IBM computer to keep everyone honest.

◊ For the senior set there was Mohawk's 1961 "Golden-Age" discount fare which offered one-third discounted fare to men over 65 and women over 62 who paid a $5 membership fee and agreed to fly after midnight and before 1300 hours. In contrast was Frontier's Youth Fare club, involving a $5.00 membership fee.

◊ Frontier's creative attempts at innovation brought it some grief from other airlines – as well as from a bus operator. In 1966, after discovering that females accounted for just 20-percent of its passengers, it announced a "Ladies' Fare," a 15-day system-wide 50percent discount. Then Western Air Lines, Northwest Airlines, and even Trailways Bus System protested to the C.A.B. that such a fare was "unduly discriminatory." A year later Frontier tried a second variation, which was again struck down despite Frontier president Lew Dymond's plea that such discounts were not discriminatory because, 'as everyone knew,' it was the men who paid for the ladies' tickets.

◊ In October, 1959 Allegheny adopted a $11.82 fare for travel between Philadelphia and Pittsburgh, Pennsylvania. It was an early version of no-frills, with passengers traveling stand-by and handling their own luggage. In April, 1961 Bonanza offered reduced-rate travel between resort cities, with a $26 roundtrip fare in the busy Los Angeles - Las Vegas market and $27 between Phoenix and Palm Springs.

◊   Some 14 months later Trans-Texas asked the C.A.B. for permission to offer the first local coach fares: passengers could get a 20% discount but only on its DC-3s, and the flights would offer only beverage service. In 1965 Central began a "Plus $10" fare which offered roundtrip travel for just $10 above the one-way fare..

◊   And of course there was Texas International's "Fly for Peanuts" campaign, which gained it national attention, especially when one ad featured the likeness of former peanut-farmer, President Jimmy Carter. Obviously, when it came to creative marketing, the cash-strapped Locals were the proven experts.

Building Stronger Routes:

Just as a 'local' commuter train or subway stops at every station, so did the Local Service Airlines, at least in their early years. A North Central route between Omaha, Nebraska and Rapid City, South Dakota had no fewer than eight intermediate stops, and not necessarily in a direct line. Some argue that this was to ensure service to every community; others say it was to protect the trunks, which could fly non-stop between the two larger cities, from competition.

But soon the C.A.B. would allow Locals to deviate from this policy. The goal was to help the fledglings, and thus to lower their break-even needs. The policy was known as 'Route Strengthening,' and it would culminate in the mid-1960s in an almost complete about-face in C.A.B. thinking.

As early as 1946 the C.A.B. decided to let Pioneer Air Lines operate a "shuttle service" between any two contingent points, as long as it offered a minimum of two such round trips daily. Three years later the Middle Atlantic Area Case gave All American (later Allegheny) entry into the New York City – Pittsburgh market as long as it served at least three of the six named intermediate points on this route.

The next big break came with the introduction of Flag Stops, which allowed a local to skip a stop if no one needed to deplane or emplane there. The first local to get this right was Southwest (later Pacific), which was burdened by having to serve many smaller communities in central California.

Then, in 1958, the Seven States Area Investigation grew the Locals' route map by allowing them to add places dropped by the trunk airlines. Almost immediately Braniff dropped 13 destinations, Western dropped seven, and United dropped four – all picked up by Locals. Then the C.A.B. sweetened the pot by ruling that Locals could now operate <u>nonstop</u> between any terminal points deemed 'non-competitive' and had to make just one intermediate stop between 'competitive' terminals. Reducing subsidy costs was the rationale for this change.

It all seemed correct to *Flight* magazine's editor/publisher, and perennial local-supporter, George Haddaway. He saw the Locals developing a dual identity. Since, he noted in 1958, it had already become "…impossible to fly via trunk airline to a nearby city at the beginning of a business day and return that evening," perhaps the Locals could "operate certain non-stop services between the largest traffic centers located fairly close together" if the C.A.B. would lift the every-stop requirement. He was prescient, but it would take another seven years for the next major overhaul to occur.

That change, coinciding with the Locals' acquisition of pure-jets, facilitated their image-makeover into "regionals," a term they now favored. But the jets drove the accounting department crazy, for they were ill-suited to the type of flying done by these airlines. For example, to operate a 200-mile non-stop with a DC-9-30 would cost $306, in 1970s dollars. But turn that trip into two legs of 100 miles apiece and suddenly the operating cost jumps dramatically, to $362, or 20 percent more. The Locals began to argue that if they had to service all stops with their new jets their costs would rise and thus would their subsidy needs.

The C.A.B. accepted their argument, announcing on December 8, 1966 that it intended to remove, as quickly as possible, restrictions that prevented the Locals from offering nonstop flights between terminals already receiving trunkline service. It called this **Nonstop Authority**, and said it was granting it because doing so would result in a reduced subsidy need and would provide the public with better service. The competition would not have too great an effect on the trunks Based on "the current prosperity of the trunkline carriers," the

C.A.B. wrote "they can easily absorb some diversion of traffic in these markets without seriously impairing their earnings." But, just to keep things on an even footing, routes that a local served non-stop would be subsidy ineligible. Not only that, but it introduced revenue-sharing: if future revenues increased faster than they did during a base period then the government would be entitled to a refund in the form of subsidy reduction.

It was a clever move. Between 1967 and 1970 the new non-stop capability resulted in greatly enhanced revenues for many Locals. By 1970, one analyst claimed, some 70 percent of Allegheny's revenue came from its new non-stop routes, even though it competed with the trunks. Mohawk estimated that non-stop routes, just 25 percent of its total route miles, generated 65 percent of its revenue.

Of course, to put this in the proper perspective, by the end of 1969 the Locals'/regionals' share of all scheduled revenue passenger miles was still below ten percent; and so they were still little more than a minor annoyance to the major airlines. Allegheny offered much greater frequency between Philadelphia and Boston than did Eastern, but an Eastern manager was philosophical about it, telling *Aviation Week*, "We can't all put in 13 round trips….If somebody makes the kind of commitment, it is more important to them and fits in their system."

Also helping was **By-pass Authority,** another bit of C.A.B. largesse which made the Locals into 'players.' One of the traditional roles of the Locals had been to bring passengers from smaller intermediate communities to a terminal point, where some passengers would then be 'fed' (hence the original name 'Feeder') to a trunk airline, which would then carry them on to a major city, perhaps an international gateway. By-Pass Authority allowed the local to carry passengers directly from an intermediate city to a major city, by-passing the terminal point entirely and keeping all the revenue for the entire trip. For example, under By-Pass, Southern got the right to fly from smaller towns like Columbus, Georgia non-stop to Washington, D.C. and New York City; North central could skip Chicago and fly directly from Milwaukee, Minnesota to New York; and Ozark could fly from Champaign-Urbana, Illinois (home of the U. of Illinois) non-stop to New York City, also by-passing Chicago.

Use It or Lose It:

Maybe the C.A.B.'s 1958 " Use It or Lose It" policy should have been called 'Put Up or Shut Up.' An attempt to reduce subsidy levels by eliminating unprofitable communities, it aimed squarely at communities deemed under-performing. The idea was to give such places a six-month grace period for residents to become aware of air service. Then, for the next year, those towns would have to board an average of five passengers per day or face an immediate review of their right to service. It turned out to be a toothless tiger.

As historians note, the only places eliminated were places that probably never should have been given service in the first place. And the episode reveals the bureaucratic side of the C.A.B. that helped convince small-government adherents that less truly was more, which sped along deregulation. For, each quarter, cities deemed under-performing received a letter which always said the same thing: (1) Here are the traffic statistics for your city and other cities receiving subsidy; (2) unless better use is made of the air service, its cost to the government is not warranted and its continuation would not be in the public interest. Compiling and sending the letters each quarter may have kept the C.A.B. staff well-employed, but they had little overall impact on load factors.

Where they did have impact was in Congress, where they provided several politicians with the opportunity to grand-stand for their constituents. For example, Senator William F. Proxmire (D., Wis.) who once created "The Golden Fleece Award" to spotlight drains on taxpayer money, rose on the floor of the Senate to vigorously defend the 80 out of 540 communities threatened with loss of service, calling them "victims of the C.A.B." And Senator Hubert Horatio Humphrey, Jr. (D., Minn.), who would be President Lyndon Johnson's Vice President and the 1968 Democratic Presidential Nominee argued that these cities had spent hundreds of millions to improve their airports and now were being foiled by a government agency.

The communities themselves pleaded innocent, arguing that the fault lay not with them but with the Local Service Airline for providing poor service; others said their lack of passenger boardings was compensated by the amount of freight they generated; and still others said they were essential to national defense. Several cities in Nebraska and Nevada sued Frontier and Bonanza to keep them from implementing the C.A.B.-approved suspensions.. All these efforts worked, because nine years after Use It or Lose It first appeared, 41 cities which technically should have been dropped were still receiving service.

Even an airline sued. In 1967 the city of Wilmington, Delaware (corporate headquarters of chemical giant E. I. du Pont de Nemours, or DuPont) was served by American, Eastern, and Allegheny. But because Wilmington boarded an average of just 1.4 passengers per day, the C.A.B. suspended Allegheny's service there. However it didn't suspend American and Eastern. So Allegheny sued. The courts ruled in favor of the C.A.B., and Allegheny's lawyers went to the U.S. Supreme Court, which refused to hear the case, effectively upholding the C.A.B.

Today Wilmington, a thriving town of some 75,000, has no air service at all. Eastern, of course, is a ghost and American dropped the city. Continental does serve it, in a unique way. It code-shares with Amtrak, which offers a 90-minute train ride from Newark Liberty International down to Wilmington.

Of course, by 1969 Use It or Lose It was no longer a high priority. With the rise of the "air-taxis" (later, commuters) the C.A.B. saw a subsidy-free way to service these towns, with better frequencies. So Use It or Lose It, the C.A.B.'s attempt to increase Locals' load factors, quietly expired, and few mourned its passing.

Now that we've finished our economics lesson, let's see how the now-maturing Locals were beginning to change.

Chapter 9: A Slight Course Deviation

By 1975, anyone watching the industry had to realize that the locals sported a very different look and feel. First, there were fewer of them. Central, Lake Central, and Mohawk were gone. Bonanza, Pacific and West Coast were combined into Air West. Somehow the others – Allegheny, Frontier, North Central, Ozark, Piedmont, Southern, and Texas International, as well as Air New England – no longer seemed like 'also-rans.'

The average person waiting for a flight at a mid-sized city airport like Denver's Stapleton or St. Louis' Lambert probably could not tell the difference between Frontier's or Ozark's jets and those operated by United or TWA, except for the color schemes. Even the term "local service" had fallen into disfavor. They now preferred to think of themselves as "regional airlines," a term prompted by their move into the intercity markets.

Which was the result of a reversal in thinking and attitude on the part of the Washington overseers (see Chapter 8: Business Class). In 1966 the C.A.B. had awarded both "by-pass" and "non-stop" authority to the locals, allowing them to expand their horizons – even, in some markets, to compete with the larger airlines. Declaring the new routes subsidy-ineligible, the Board hoped that these profitable markets would allow the locals to then 'cross-subsidize' or 'self-subsidize' their less profitable markets, just as the trunks had been doing for years.

Instead the profits from these new markets encouraged the locals to purchase even more jets. But they were still stuck with the need to serve those less-profitable markets.

Take Frontier. It served 16 states —one-third of the continental U.S., but those states were thinly populated, with many smaller places. *Flight* magazine noted that 42 of its destinations were producing as few as 20 passengers per day. *Newsweek* observed that of Frontier's 94 destinations (a) 88 were still subsidized, and (b) 57 were draining money– a whopping $21M from 1968 to 1971. Frontier's President Al Feldman claimed 70 percent of Frontier's revenue came from just 14 percent of its destinations. He told *Aviation Daily*, "It's got to be a hell of a note when we can make a living competing with United, Braniff, Continental and Western but we can't make a living being a monopoly carrier flying to communities which should have air service."

Under deregulation, airlines are able to drop service to unprofitable destinations. But deregulation had not yet happened, and so a different solution was needed. Thanks to a late 1960's C.A.B. policy decision, air taxi or commuter airlines, which then numbered more than 200, were permitted to substitute for both the trunks and the locals at unprofitable places. As a result, by 1975 the locals served 38 fewer places than in 1970, mostly places with populations less than 50,000. Those places were now served by commuters, which then 'fed' these passengers to the locals. How ironic – the airlines that had begun life as feeders now had their own feeders.

The first was Allegheny, which on November 15, 1967 began Allegheny Commuter Airlines, using airplanes supplied by Henson Flying Service, operating as The Hagerstown Commuter. Hagerstown, a city in Maryland some 65 miles northwest of Washington, D.C., was home to Richard (Dick) Henson, a long-time pilot and chairman of its Aviation Commission. Today Hagerstown Regional Airport is also known as Richard A. Henson Field; but, ironically, as of September, 2007 it has had no scheduled airline service (see Chapter 11, "Ground Stopped").

Henson had grown dissatisfied with what he viewed as Allegheny's dismal service, so in April, 1962 he began his own air-taxi service with two light twins: a bright yellow Beech D-18 and an Aero Commander, plus a Beech Bonanza as backup. By 1965 he was turning a nice profit, spurring Allegheny to obtain a Beech 18 in order to compete. But Allegheny, bound by Part 121 of the Federal Air Regulations, had to use two pilots on that airplane, rendering it much less profitable. So Allegheny's president Leslie Barnes made Henson an offer: would he be willing to operate Hagerstown service not to Washington National but to Baltimore and Hazelton, Pennsylvania, The name would be changed to Allegheny Commuter Airlines. Henson would provide the airplanes while Allegheny would provide the other services, including marketing. Henson accepted the offer, marking the first-ever such arrangement between a large airline and a smaller air-taxi operator, and the first flights began in November, 1967.

In one year boardings doubled, to 12,300 passengers. This so impressed the C.A.B. that it agreed to substitute Allegheny Commuter for the local at five additional points: Salisbury, Maryland; Hazelton and Dubois, Pennsylvania; Danville, Illinois; and Mansfield, Ohio. By the end of 1969 all six cities were showing increased boardings, and Allegheny needed some $324,000 less subsidy annually. Also, in November, 1969 Allegheny added a second Allegheny Commuter partner – Ransome Airlines – on its Philadelphia – Washington, D.C. run. By the end of 1974 twelve airlines operated under the Allegheny Commuter umbrella; besides Dick Henson's and J. Dawson Ransome's companies there were: AeroMech, Air North, Atlantic City Airlines, Chautauqua Airlines, Clark Aviation, Crown Airways, Fisher Brothers Aviation, Pocono Airlines, Suburban Airlines, and Vercoa Air Service. The annual passenger boardings for the 12 combined exceeded one million.

But not all attempts worked out as well. A similar attempt probably helped kill off Mohawk. Early in 1970 the CAB approved the " Mohawk Commuter Package," under which Air North, then operating as " Mohawk Commuter," was allowed to replace Mohawk at three locations and supplement it at eight others in upstate New York. Those cities had been eking out an average ten boardings per day – terrible for Mohawk's 44-seat FH-227Bs but adequate for Air North's 18-seat de Haviland DHC-6 Twin Otters. Air North's break-even load factor was just 43-percent, so everyone was quite happy with the arrangement. Everyone, that is, except Mohawk's pilots.

They viewed this early version of outsourcing as a potential loss of jobs. The local chapter of the pilots' union demanded veto power of any further decisions, but Mohawk refused. That precipitated a 154-day strike, which then held the record for shutdown of an airline by a labor dispute. The union eventually agreed to binding arbitration, but, seriously hurt by the strike and other economic blows, Mohawk soon announced that it had agreed to be acquired by Allegheny.

Other locals turned not to outsourcing but to airplanes even smaller than the DC-3 to serve the less-profitable cities. In July, 1966 West Coast introduced its ' Miniliners' – six-place twin-engine Piper PA-23 Aztecs, to light-traffic cities like Roseburg, Oregon, or Twin Falls, Idaho. The Aztecs were eventually replaced by eight-seat Piper PA-31 Navajos, painted in the colors of Air West. For many years those Navajos provided Sun Valley, Idaho and similar towns with service to bigger cities such as Boise, Idaho or Salt Lake City, Utah until Air West dropped the routes entirely.

Out in Denver, Frontier also used light-twins, after a brief dalliance with outsourcing. In 1970 Arizona-based Apache Airlines began service to a group of unprofitable North Dakota and Montana cities. Within six months Apache was bleeding red ink, some $300,000 worth, and was seeking to bail out of the agreement. Its president became almost-paranoid, alleging some sort of sabotage by residents hoping to bring Frontier back.

By November, 1970 the residents did have Frontier back. It had leased two de Havilland Canada DHC-6 Twin Otters and based them in Great Falls, Montana, from where the rugged high-wing turboprops operated one daily roundtrip over two separate route segments that had once been operated with DC-3s. Frontier also operated 15-seat Beech 99s to the tiny Western Nebraska towns of Sidney, Chadron, and Alliance, to replace the Convair 580 twice-daily roundtrips.

Those Convair 580s would play a significant role more than a decade later in an outsourcing venture called Frontier Commuter. Combs Airways acquired nine of them in a lease-purchase agreement and began serving six towns – three in Wyoming and three in Colorado – on October 17, 1983. Startup problems caused Combs to eventually default on its payments; Frontier demanded its airplanes; and Combs filed for bankruptcy. Wyoming electronics millionaire Nick Kondur, who had been financially supporting commuter airline Excellair (formerly Air US) switched allegiances, allowing Excellair to fold, and put almost $1 million into rejuvenating Frontier Commuter. By October, 1984 Frontier Commuter had added seven cities and two new states. It provided many of Frontier's dropped cities, including little North Platte and Scotts Bluff, Nebraska as well as the larger Omaha and Lincoln with service to Denver, where passengers would connect with either Frontier or Frontier Horizon, Frontier's short-lived attempt at a non-union business travelers' airline.

Texas International briefly experimented with Beech 99A's, which it called "Skylarks," operating them to places like the east Texas town of Lufkin, 120 miles northeast of Houston and "Crossroads of the Piney Woods" or the Texas Gulf Coast town of Victoria, some 80 miles southwest of Houston. The experiment lasted from early 1970 to 1972.

Another short-lived in-house experiment was Ozark's flirtation with the de Havilland Canada DHC-6 Twin Otter, leased in 1972 from Florida's Mackey International Airlines to compete with rival Air Illinois's service to Chicago's downtown Meigs Field. By 1974 Oark had terminated that service, possibly because it couldn't win concessions from its pilots for flying smaller aircraft. Eleven years later, in October 1985, Ozark would outsource with Air Midwest to operate Fairchild Metroliners under the " Ozark Midwest" label.

Thus, by 1975, the locals were by no means the same type of airline they had been ten years earlier. Now they were truly regionals, operating equipment identical to that of the trunks and in some cases competing with them. They still served the smaller communities, but not as well. In 1962 they had been certificated at 477 points. By 1975 that number had dropped to just 380.

Then came deregulation. The Airline Deregulation Act of 1978 made it easier to enter or exit markets. Frontier was quick to take advantage . Between 1979 and 1982 it dropped 36 smaller communities and added 29 new destinations. The discontinued places included smaller towns like Wolf Point, Montana or Gallup, New Mexico while the places added were major cities like Detroit and Seattle. Frontier worked hard to apply the proper spin, claiming the deleted cities would all be better served by commuter carriers "able to offer increased frequencies in short-haul markets."

But that spin did little to impress people impacted. A *Denver Post* story focused on the town of Cortez, 261 miles from Denver in southwest Colorado. Before the service cuts, Cortez had three daily departures to Denver and two to Albuquerque, New Mexico. Some 10,000 residents had made use of those flights the previous year. But now, "With little bus and no rail service," the story noted, "total elimination of air service would mean a drive to Durango, two mountain passes and 60 miles away, or to Farmington, New Mexico, about the same distance." Those making the drive could then travel aboard a de Havilland Canada DHC-6 Twin Otter or a Fairchild Metroliner – both a far cry from Frontier's larger, sturdier, and more comfortable Convair 580s.

Little wonder that some claimed the locals had forgotten their roots. Others asserted that they were simply taking advantage of opportunities put in place by government policy. Either way, by the end of 1979 the surviving locals were 'players' in the domestic aviation scene. And they were very different from the quaint little airlines that had struggled to emerge, as a butterfly struggles to emerge from its chrysalis, in the 1950s.

But even the most beautiful butterfly eventually dies; and our next chapter will trace the final years of the Locals.

Chapter 10: Off the Radar Scope

Sadly, the locals are gone. And in today's deregulated market-driven industry – what with legacy carriers in and out of bankruptcy and seeking to merge, with low-cost carriers carrying at least one-quarter of all domestic passengers, and with service to smaller communities becoming less and less common (see Chapter 11: Ground Stopped) – it's almost hard to believe that the locals ever did exist.

But they did – some for as long as four decades – and it is the goal of this chapter to trace, in chronological order, the final flights of those thirteen locals which received permanent certification in 1955, as well as latecomer Air New England. As for the all-too-brief fate of pioneering Pioneer, the full story surrounding its premature demise is covered in Chapter 4: "A Change of Planes."

Central Absorbed by Frontier - September 1, 1967

It was quick, neat, and clean. And it all made sense to the C.A.B. examiners. In June, 1967, Frontier, already operating pure-jets (three Boeing 727s) and serving ten western states, proposed acquiring the much smaller and less profitable Central, which served just six states and whose most modern airplane was the Convair 600, the Rolls-Royce Dart-powered version of the venerable Convair 340.

Frontier's revenue was more than double Central's, as were its expenses. But its break-even need was smaller, leaving it with a post-subsidy net income almost triple that of Central's. Frontier argued that there would be savings from the "common use of personnel, facilities, and equipment" – even though it would later put those Convair 600s up for sale. Frontier also promised that no Central employee would be harmed and that they would be paid at Frontier's rates. The C.A.B. examiner thought the merged systems would bring better service and that there was no danger of a monopoly.

The examiner announced his findings on August 2, 1967 and a month later the deal was consummated. Although the combined route systems made Frontier the largest local at the time, it didn't merit much more than a 21-line story on the back page of *The New York Times*, below the local weather map. Ironically, another aviation story received the more prominent top-of-page position; the previous day had marked the 40th anniversary of the first transcontinental mail/ passenger service.

Bonanza + Pacific + West Coast = Air West - April 17, 1968

Nick Bez always did believe that his airline should serve that entire coast whose name it flaunted. But the C.A.B. thought otherwise, allowing West Coast's route map to extend only as far south as Medford, Oregon. The rest of Oregon and all of California was served by Pacific. In 1963 Bez bought a third of Pacific's stock, but the threat of an investigation by the C.A.B.'s Enforcement Division gave him second thoughts and he sold his shares.

Finally, in 1967, with Pacific suffering heavy losses and West Coast facing falling profits, the mutually-beneficial merger became a three-way deal, with Bonanza joining. Stockholders of all three gave approval to create a new airline, Air West. Bez became Chairman and CEO while Bonanza's Ed Converse became Vice-Chairman and Pacific's Robert G. Henry would be President. The Air West route map would include 94 communities (38 from West Coast, 38 from Pacific, and 19 from Bonanza) – actually giving it a regional presence.

That concept – regional service – figured prominently in the C.A.B. examiner's decision. He wrote that it would change the role of the local service airlines, from many carriers each serving a small localized area to a few carriers serving large parts of the nation. That progressive view meshed perfectly with that of Nick Bez, Jr., who believed that regional service would allow a businessman in Boise, who may have once considered Salt Lake City to be his principal community of interest, to instead view San Francisco or Los Angeles as a natural part of his marketing area. But the idea of a new regional competitor didn't sit well with Western Air Lines, which showed up with a gaggle of experts arguing against the merger lest the public somehow confuse Air West with Western Airlines. Bez produced his own experts, and the C.A.B. examiner overturned Western's argument, noting that: no one had ever confused the earlier West Coast with Western.

The C.A.B. approved the merger on February 23, 1968, but, because the airline would also serve parts of Canada, the merger required President Johnson's approval. That came on April 4, 1968, and, as of April 17, 1968 the three locals were officially a new regional. But it was facing a lot of turbulence.

In the next three years things went from gloomy to gloomier, despite the bright desert-inspired paint jobs on the airplanes' exteriors. Net income for 1968 was a <u>negative</u> $11 million, 1969's was negative $20.8 million, and 1970's fell to negative $32m. That's when the famed Howard Hughes offered to purchase Air West's assets for $94 million and assume its liabilities. His infusions of cash kept the airline alive while the C.A.B. pondered his offer. Eventually Air West's stockholders received not the originally-offered $22 per share but just $9 per share.

The stockholders squawked, but Hughes, who once owned TWA, again had an airline. His management team drove it into a profitability streak that lasted from 1971 through 1978. They sold the Piper Navajos, most Fairchild F-27s, and the Boeing 727-100s (from Pacific). Then, between 1972 and 1974 they spent $46 million on 17 used DC-9s. In 1975 they spent another $36m on three new Boeing 727-200s. The garish yellow paint scheme prompted the marketing people to call the airline "The Top Banana in the West."

But in 1979 a two-month strike by reservations and other office staff plus attempts to compete in a now-deregulated environment caused a $22 million loss, unacceptable to the bean-counters in the Hughes organization (he had passed in April, 1976). They began looking for ways to cut their losses, and found Republic Airlines, the one-year old created by the merger of North Central and Southern (see below). They sold <u>Hughes Air west</u> for some $38.5 million. On October 1, 1980 Republic formally acquired Hughes Air West, whose 53 destinations brought Republic's total to 200 cities served, actually more than any other domestic airline of the time. Exactly six years later, Republic would become part of Northwest.

Lake Central Absorbed Into Allegheny - July 1, 1968

It was another of those arrangements that just seemed to make sense to all concerned, including the stockholders, the city representatives who came to testify, and – most importantly – the C.A.B. examiner, who noted that Lake Central had long been beset by problems while Allegheny was "a stable and well-managed carrier." The respective fleets showed this. Allegheny had 49 airplanes including Douglas DC-9s, Convair 580s, and Fairchild F-27Js. Lake Central's fleet, half as large, consisted of just ten Convair 580s, a Convair 340, and 12 trouble-plagued Nord-262s.

The examiner liked the idea of a merger. First, he wrote, it would result in a $1 million reduction in subsidy need. Second, the employees would not suffer since Allegheny had promised employment to the Lake Central people "to the greatest extent possible." Third, the merger would result in "first single-plane service, new competitive services, and upgrading of service with better equipment."

In short, the merger was consistent with C.A.B. policy "of favoring the combination of a weak local carrier – in this case, Lake Central – with a strong one." The agency accepted its examiners findings and ordered that, effective July 1, 1968, the two certificates be merged into one.

Mohawk Is Absorbed by Allegheny - April 6, 1972

It didn't seem possible that colorful quiky Mohawk should find itself in such dire straits. The airline had been an innovator: first local to operate pure jets, first U.S. carrier to hire an African-American as a stewardess, and the only local to operate a helicopter subsidiary. But by 1971 the airline was definitely not well.

It had been rocked by the recession of 1970. Then a strike at General Electric, a major employer in Mohawk's service area, caused a substantial loss of business traveler revenue. But the worst blow was a 154-day pilots' strike, which saw the airline furloughing almost 90-percent of its workforce. Its loss of almost $12 million in 1970 compounded its 1968 deficit of $3.3 million and its 1969 deficit of $4.7 million. By April the striking pilots had agreed to submit their demands to binding arbitration and Mohawk resumed service on April 13, 1971.

One day later it revealed that it had agreed to be acquired by Allegheny, at that time the largest local. For its part Mohawk would receive a cash infusion that would help reduce outstanding debt and debt-repayment schedules. For its part, Allegheny wound up with a route system of some 11,000 miles, extended from Toronto and Montreal, Canada as far south as Memphis, Tennessee and as far west as St. Louis, Missouri.

The merger, proposed by Allegheny, had been simmering for four months as both sides haggled over details. Finally, on April 14, both Boards of Directors approved the details. Mohawk's relatively-new President Stephenson said the deal was "the best economic alternative available at this time." Unfortunately Mohawk's 16-year president Robert E. Peach, unable to deal with his beloved airline's disappearance, committed suicide.

Less personally involved, the C.A.B. examiner called the idea "a sound business decision." It would end Mohawk's financial troubles as well as provide improved service, lower subsidy need, etc. In its ruling the full Board heartily concurred with its examiner, praising Allegheny for its seamless absorption of Lake Central in 1968 and arguing that the Mohawk absorption would create a more profitable Allegheny, which, in turn, would lower that airline's subsidy needs. It also noted that Mohawk's employees would be adequately buffered from economic blows, including layoffs, an altruistic concern and quaint by today's standards.

The C.A.B. ordered the transfer to Allegheny of Mohawk's certificates for Routes 72 and 94. Because of Mohawk's routes into Canada that decision required presidential approval, which President Nixon gave on April 6, 1972 and the airline of "Little Moh" and the Air Chiefs ceased to exist.

North Central and Southern Form Republic - June 4, 1979

"...A good clean marriage" was how North Central's vice-president for finance described his company's planned takeover of Southern. As in many marriages, one partner is stronger. Here it was North Central. Compared to Southern's, its fleet was larger (56 vs. 38), its yearly revenue was larger ($299 million vs. $188.5 million), and its net income a whopping ten times larger ($22.2 million vs. $2.4 million).

Southern's founder and President Frank Hulse welcomed the idea. He told a *New York Times* reporter that merger might offer the success that had eluded Southern in its three decade history. The recent years had been a roller coaster ride, with 1978 profit falling to $2.4 million from the previous year's $9.3 million. Part of the problem was the competition from Delta and Eastern and their discount fares. Yet Southern was by no means a basket case. Its route map included 50 cities in 17 states, plus the Cayman Islands.

But Hulse knew that impressive statistics are no substitute for revenue. He had already made overtures to both Piedmont and Texas International when big handsome North Central arrived on the scene. North Central was certainly strong; its net income had grown impressively in 1977 and 1978, making it, according to *The New York Times*, "a textbook case on what freedom from government regulation can do for a business." Most of the credit, the paper said, belonged to the airline's new long legs, with its jets pairing cities like Detroit with Boston and Milwaukee with Miami, even though it still served most of its smaller and medium-sized communities.

In so many, ways, the *Times* story said, the two airlines were a perfect fit. Their routes did not overlap, and a combined route structure would provide passengers with their first through-plane service between the South and the Upper Midwest. And, as one industry observer told *The Wall Street Journal,* with deregulation now a reality, the only hope for smaller airlines who wanted to attract investors was to combine themselves and grow.

It also made sense to the C.A.B., which in February, 1979 still had some say in such matters. The merger was advised, its Administrative Law Judge wrote, because it would give United, Delta, and Northwest some healthy competition while providing better service for residents of the smaller communities. Neither the Justice Department nor the Transportation Department offered any opposition. The usual bureaucratic slowness prevailed, and it wasn't until June that the matter was finally on its way to the White House, a required step because of Southern's service to Grand Cayman Island. President Carter signed the order on June 4, 1979, thus creating Republic, the nation's 13th largest airline.

Republic prospered and grew. It acquired Hughes Airwest in 1980 (see above) and five years later had a 169-airplane fleet, including Boeing 757s, plus its own feeder system, Republic Express, which had come online at the end of May 1985. But 1985 would be Republic's last year as an independent airline. Northwest had come bearing money, and on October 1, 1986 Republic became part of Northwest, effectively doubling the size of that airline's workforce.

Air New England Expires - October 31, 1981

The very last local to be certified, on January 20, 1975, this scrappy carrier's relatively short existence helped prove yet again that the New England region can be as resistant to airline profitability as its rocky soil was resistant to those first farmers' plows. There were several reasons. First, the region is a paradox. The southern part of New England (from the New York / Connecticut border north to Boston) is a compact and bustling area with at least nine cities of 100,000 or more population, which should generate lots of passengers. However, the cities are relatively close and the area features both excellent highways and adequate rail service. The northern part is much more rural, but its cities, although spread further apart, offer 'low market potential.'

To make matters worse, Air New England had lots of competition from the many third-level airlines, including Nor East Commuter, the carrier formed by Air New England founder, Joseph C. Whitney, after he had been forced out. By 1978 seven commuter airlines were competing directly with Air New England. One historian suggested that the area was jinxed, because no airline had ever been totally successful in the region, even with subsidy.

That was a fact that rapidly became apparent to Air New England's management. Despite a subsidy of $3.8 million, the year 1978 ended with a loss of half as much, or $1.9 million. The next year's loss was $2.1 million, and a combination of bad weather and labor unrest was beginning to make the airline appear so dysfunctional that *Time* magazine ridiculed it in a story entitled "Destination Doubtful."

The final year was a classic example of good news – bad news. Air New England had purchased two Convair 580s and had added such non-New England cities as Baltimore and Cleveland to its route map. But the new routes had lots of pure-jet competition from the bigger airlines. Plus the Professional Air Traffic Controllers (PATCO) history-making strike was about to disrupt air travel, especially in the congested northeast.

Even though management had wrangled a ten-percent pay concession and was actively seeking a merger partner, time ran out. On October 31, 1981 Air New England shut down forever.

Texas International "Disappears" - October 31, 1982

Mention the name Frank Lorenzo in any gathering of airline industry veterans and you're sure to get a reaction. Despite the endless controversies, few can deny that, for a while, Lorenzo did manage to turn an ailing local into a financial, and media, success. But then he folded it into a larger entity, leaving no trace of its colorful past.

The story begins in the latter half of the 1960s (long before Lorenzo's arrival on the scene) when TTA (Trans-Texas Airlines) was desperately trying to change its "TreeTop Airways" / "TinkerToy Airways" image.

Some heavy spending was involved. First came the 1965 decision to re-engine the Convair 240s with Rolls-Royce Dart turbines, making them Convair 600s "Silver Clouds." The cost came to $15 million. Then TTA, like other locals, began ordering pure-jets, DC-9-10s, to compete with Braniff's Lockheed 188 Electra turboprops and Boeing 720Bs at major Texas cities like Dallas and Houston. The price tag for the first six DC-9s was a hefty $50 million.

Those expenses began to affect the bottom line, and, despite increases in revenue, TTA began showing net losses in 1967. Things got progressively worse. Another name change, this time to Texas International (TXI) in April of 1969, and a route from Albuquerque to Los Angeles impressed the public but not the accountants, who saw that the airline was in deep trouble. By 1971 TXI had a negative $7 million net worth and was about to be placed in receivership.

How did Lorenzo get involved? Some say TXI shareholder Donald Burr (who would later found PEOPLExpress) argued for Lorenzo, and others claim it was Chase Manhattan Bank that wanted Lorenzo brought in to study TXI's problems. For Lorenzo's Jet Capital Corporation the deal was a lucrative one, paying $15,000 <u>per month</u> in consultant fees. For Lorenzo the deal was even better, as he managed to wind up with 59 percent of the voting rights even though he owned only 26 percent of the stock.

Then Lorenzo asked the C.A.B. to approve him as TXI's new owner, which it did in October 1972. He set about making TXI well again, persuading creditors to hold off and restructuring TXI's debt. He also took a hard look at the route map, trying to maximize the more profitable destinations and reduce exposure in the thinner markets. By the end of 1973 TXI had eked out a small profit of $319,000, and $401,000 the next year. But that was a mere pittance compared to the following year's losses of some $4 million, caused, in part, by an 18-week strike that grounded the airline. In retrospect the strike foreshadowed Lorenzo's later anti-union machinations; it was provoked by his demand that ticket agents and others do between 20- to 30percent of their work as part-timers. Lorenzo used Mutual Aid Pact funds to wait out the workers, who finally gave up in April 1975.

The airline muddled along much as it had before, a minor player even among locals. Then in 1977 an idea that today seems ordinary but then was almost revolutionary brought it national attention. According to the airline history *Rapid Descent,* the idea came from then- C.A.B. Chairman John Robson, eager to see if the pro- deregulation forces were correct and that reducing fares would spur travel. With Lorenzo at their backs, TXI's marketing people came up with the now historic ' Peanuts' fares, offering a flat 50 percent off one flight each day in previously poor markets. Ads featuring a cartoon-like President Jimmy Carter as the Georgia peanut farmer he had once been below the words "Everybody should be able to fly for Peanuts" drew media attention and, more important, profits.

But Lorenzo wasn't content to be a little fish. Deregulation's implications scared him; he believed that a little fish like TXI could be devoured by the bigger fish. The only protection was for little Texas International to grow itself – by swallowing up some larger fish – whether or not they welcomed his advances. He launched the airline industry's first-ever hostile takeover attempt, buying up approximately ten percent of National, an airline four times the size of TXI.

Technically he lost out to Pan Am, which agreed to purchase the Sun King for $350 million, or $41 per share. But Lorenzo walked away with a pre-tax profit of $46 million, a tidy nest-egg for the next attempt. That was a brief foray against TWA, ironically his first employer. In late 1979, with a five-percent share in the venerable carrier, he tried to persuade TWA's parent, Trans World Corporation, that TXI could provide a Houston hub and access to Mexico – a perfect fit for the international airline. Trans World's chairman figuratively laughed in Lorenzo's face and literally walked out of their breakfast meeting.

After TWA rejected his offer, which included TXI's DC-9s, Lorenzo found a better use for them. In 1980 he had them repainted a shockingly-bright red, with a stylized 'Big Apple' logo on the tail, and thus had a fleet for his newest venture, New York Air, which would be the first major non-union U.S. airline. He planned to compete with Eastern's lucrative Boston – NYC –Washington shuttle, and possibly compete with his ex-friend Don Burr's PEOPLExpress, which had yet to fly. And he created Texas Air Corporation as a "shell holding company… which became the parent of both TXI and New York Air."

He also had a secret. All this time he had quietly been buying shares in Continental. Because the respected carrier had fallen on hard times, he was able to get them cheaply, in the $13 range. With almost a 50-percent stake, Lorenzo announced his intentions in 1980, starting a nasty battle. Continental fought back with press releases and appeals to the Securities and Exchange Commission. Its employees pledged to pool their funds to try to beat his offer. But it was a losing battle, and it cost the life of Continental's Alvin (Al) Feldman, who had come to the airline from Frontier. Unable to bear the thought of Lorenzo's acquiring Continental and already despondent over the loss of his wife, Feldman committed suicide on August 9, 1981. Ironically, he was just two years older than Robert E. Peach, Mohawk's former CEO, had been when he shot himself over his beloved airline's acquisition (see above).

But major corporate acquisitions cannot be halted for a mere suicide. On November 25, 1981 the board of directors approved the concept and eight months later, on July 15, 1982, the stockholders followed suit. Anticipating that approval, the two airlines had begun issuing dual timetables on June 1, 1982. The official date for ex- feeder Texas International to formally acquire small trunk Continental was October 31, 1982.

Outsiders may not have been clear as to exactly who had absorbed whom, for Continental became the surviving entity. TXI's airplanes were repainted in Continental's colors, and the name Texas International disappeared forever.

Frontier is Forced to Stop Flying - August 24, 1986

In 1982 Frontier seemed to have a promising future. It operated an all-jet fleet – Boeing 737s, with McDonnell Douglas MD-80s on order.

To an outsider, all looked fine. But in just four years the airline would be gone, the victim of deregulation, or broken promises, or both.

The accountants saw it first. The $6 million loss for 1982 was Frontier's first in ten years, but not its last. Ironically, thanks to deregulation, its original Denver – Salt Lake City gravy route was open to competition from seven other airlines. At its Denver hub the airline was being squeezed by United, which had more than tripled its capacity, and by Frank Lorenzo's Continental, which was offering ridiculously low fares. Frontier President Ryland called it "an accordian type squeeze," but no one liked the tune being played. Frontier's losses for 1983 were more than double those for 1982. A short-lived experiment with a non-union budget subsidiary – Frontier Horizon – had not only failed but had caused dissent and rancor among the once-cohesive Frontier family. Small wonder that the majority stockholder, GenCorp (previously General Tire and Rubber) was actively seeking a buyer.

The logical buyer was the Frontier employees, but their first attempt at creating an ESOP (Employee Stock Ownership Plan) fell apart. By the time they were ready with a new offer of $17 per share they had competition; Frank Lorenzo was offering $20 per share. Lorenzo was hated not only as a union-buster but as being somehow responsible for ex- Frontier president Al Feldman's suicide (see TXI above). The unions sought a savior. That someone was PEOPLExpress's Don Burr, who believed that Frontier's frequent flyer program, Denver hub, and CRS (Computerized Res. System) would solve PEOPLE's problems. He countered Lorenzo's new $22 per share offer with an offer of $24 per share. In early October, 1985 Frontier's Board accepted Burr's offer, making Frontier a part of PEOPLExpress.

It wasn't one of Burr's better ideas. Besides angering his own people with the job guarantees he had offered Frontier's employees, he discovered that grafting the PEOPLE image onto Frontier, i.e. converting a full-service airline into a no-frills operation caused customers to depart in droves. Lowering prices simply sparked a three-way fare war with United and Continental. When a bean-counter showed him the sad numbers Burr angrily dismissed him, telling him to come back when he had something about which to smile.

But "smiley-faces," that 1970s cultural icon, were no longer in vogue. Frontier's losses had mounted to $10 million per month, adding to PEOPLE's distress. In the first six months of 1986 that airline had gone from black to red ink and the Directors were asking for Burr's resignation. He announced that PEOPLE was for sale, either the whole thing or any part.

We'll take the Frontier portion, said United. It offered only $146 million, half of what Burr had paid but double Frontier's net asset value. That sum would give it not only Frontier's 737s but, more importantly, more gates at congested Denver-Stapleton. It was an opportunity to drive competitor Continental out of the Mile High City, once and for all. But, said United, the deal must be completed by August 31.

Meanwhile, Lorenzo offered not only to buy Frontier but to mend fences with his former buddy Burr, suggesting a post at Texas Air. PEOPLE's directors, already openly at odds with Burr, voted to go with the United offer.

Bad move. The United deal would never materialize, and thus PEOPLE would never make back any of the costs for Frontier. The reason why still causes arguments. Some blame the seniority concerns expressed by United's pilots while others blame United, claiming it deliberately delayed the start of negotiations because it had never been serious about the purchase in the first place. Negotiations stumbled along until August 23, while the losses continued.

Finally, on August 24, 1986 PEOPLExpress shut Frontier down, announcing that if United didn't come through on its original purchase agreement they'd start bankruptcy proceedings. United's response was curt: Frontier, they said, is no longer an airline, and so we're no longer interested. On August 28, 1986 – just three months short of its 40th anniversary, Frontier was placed into Chapter Eleven bankruptcy protection.

In the end Lorenzo obtained what he had wanted. On October 17, 1986, a federal bankruptcy judge approved the $158 million sale of Frontier's assets to Lorenzo's Texas Air Corporation. The Texas Air press release gleefully announced that Continental, "a Texas Air subsidiary," would begin flying 40 ex- Frontier aircraft as early as November 1, 1986. A month later PEOPLE itself would be gone, acquired by the ever-voracious Frank Lorenzo.

Ozark Acquired by TWA - October 27, 1986

Many say it never should have been allowed to happen. Ozark was a survivor – a strong regional with a loyal customer base and a rock-solid risk-averse management. But this was the mid-1980s: corporate 'raiders' were not just media darlings but their machinations were aided by an administration with a *laissez-faire attitude toward government intervention*.

Ozark – whose 1984 profit was $12.7 million – was the second biggest airline at Lambert St. Louis International, and thus a great target. TWA's new owner, Carl Icahn, offered $19 per share, or some $225 million. His bid made sense to Ozark's Board of Directors, concerned by Ozark's comparatively poor 1985 performance.

The deal would be such a win for TWA that later Icahn was heard to boast, "We own St. Louis." It would give the venerable airline a fortress hub position, with 75-percent of Lambert's gates plus 50 well-maintained DC-9s and all the other assets of a healthy and respected airline.

But, observers wondered, would the government approve such a competition-reducing deal? One government agency, the Department of Justice, said the merger should be disapproved because it would "reduce competition (as well as raise fares and reduce service) in 68 markets emanating from St. Louis". But another agency, the Department of Transportation, disagreed. Although its Administrative Law Judge admitted that the two airlines did have a "very substantial" overlap of routes, he argued, "it cannot be shown that the merger would substantially reduce competition … or to be contrary to the public interest because other airlines are free to expand or begin service at St. Louis."

The ultimate decision remained with Elizabeth Dole, then-Secretary of Transportation. A week earlier she had approved Northwest's acquisition of competitor Republic, and few believed she would object. She didn't, rubber-stamping in early-September what some have called "the most egregious" of all the airline deals that went through in the 1980s.

Even worse than the effect on the St. Louis area was the effect on employees. Unlike the C.A.B. which had always insisted protections for the affected employees, the Administrative Law Judge argued that Ozark's people "could protect themselves … through collective bargaining." He obviously under-estimated the new management. As a 1986 headline in *The Wall Street Journal* read: " Ozark's pilots vote to merge their seniority with TWA pilots; effect is a 24-percent pay reduction."

Carl Icahn wasn't taking any reductions. He sold the entire Ozark fleet and then leased it back, effectively regaining the $240 million he had spent for Ozark. Then, by totally absorbing Ozark into TWA, he effectively obliterated Ozark's pension plan. As of October 27, 1986, the proud airline of "Three Swallows" and " Go-Getter Bird" fame, ceased to exist.

Piedmont Acquired by USAir - August 5, 1989

Piedmont was the most popular girl at the dance. *The New York Times* had called it "one of the fastest-growing and most profitable carriers in the deregulated airline industry." Now this desirable trophy was being pursued not just by another airline but by a railroad -- Norfolk Southern.

The wrangling between airline and railroad simply drove Piedmont stock higher. Norfolk Southern's holding company had offered $65 per share, all-cash. USAir's had offered more –$71 per share in stock – but Piedmont was favoring Norfolk because that offer, not requiring Department of Transportation approval, was cleaner. Piedmont's share price climbed to $69.75.

USAir really needed Piedmont, as that airline's strong presence in the American Southeast would strengthen USAir's defenses against Eastern, recently acquired by Frank Lorenzo's Texas Air Corporation. USAir feared low-cost competition from Eastern in the smaller city markets that had been USAir's bread and butter.

Complicating matters was Carl Icahn's offer of $1.65 billion for USAir, which rejected the offer and accused Icahn of trying to ruin the proposed Piedmont deal. Wall Street suspected an even more sinister motive – that Icahn was actually looking to have USAir buy moneylosing TWA. Some claim he was hinting at a three-way merger between TWA, Piedmont, and USAir.

USAir appealed to the courts. A Federal District judge issued a restraining order preventing Icahn from buying any additional USAir stock. The Department of Transportation ruled Icahn's application for USAir flawed. The Securities and Exchange Commission (SEC) got into the act, investigating Icahn's investment activities and effectively stopping him.

This gave USAir and Piedmont time to work out a deal. On March 9, 1987 Piedmont accepted USAir's offer of $69 per share, an all-cash deal worth $1.59 billion. It would require shareholder approval and sign-off by the Department of Transportation.

Which was not a sure thing. USAir and Piedmont operated at 57 airports in common and offered service to 21 identical markets. Fearing a negative response, USAir's C.E.O. Colodny went ballistic, screaming that the same judge had already approved the Republic and the Ozark acquisitions and that it would be "a travesty" if this merger did not happen.

He needn't have worried. Former Transportation Secretary Dole had already stepped down to help her husband, Senator Robert Dole's, presidential campaign. On October 30, 1987 her assistant secretary approved the merger. He would later boast that he had had to overrule his staff's tremendous opposition.

And so, on August 5, 1989, 41-year Piedmont disappeared. Its fleet totaled almost 200 aircraft, including six Boeing 767-200s, operating trans-Atlantic to London. Now all of that would become part of USAir, giving that airline the title of sole surviving local.

US Airways, Survivor

The first six decades had been pretty good! By 1999, 60 years after beginning life as a contracted mail carrier snatching mailbags strung between two poles, the airline had:

- Acquired three other locals (Lake Central, Mohawk, and Piedmont) as well as California intrastate carrier PSA.
- Expanded Piedmont's Charlotte – London trans-Atlantic service to six major European cities.
- Re-branded the Trump Shuttle as the US Airways Shuttle, servicing the lucrative New York – Washington and New York – Boston markets.
- Renamed itself yet again, this time to US Airways, created a totally new color scheme, and ordered Airbus A319s and A320s.
- Made arrangements with no fewer than ten regional carriers for code-share feeder operations as US

Airways Express at its three hubs: Pittsburgh, Philadelphia, and Charlotte.

- Created MetroJet, a short-lived low-fare carrier on the East Coast.

Then came the new century, and with it the twin blows of an economic recession plus the effects of 9/11. U.S. Airways and United considered a merger, but Department of Transportation objections prevented that from happening. Both subsequently filed for Chapter 11 bankruptcy protection from creditors. In March, 2003 U.S. Airways emerged from its first bankruptcy filing, hoping to operate leaner and more efficiently. A new obstacle was the surging popularity of low cost carriers such as AirTran, JetBlue, and, especially, Southwest, which began serving both Philadelphia and Pittsburgh – both US Airways traditional hubs –in early 2004. On September 12, 2004 U.S. Airways again filed for Chapter 11 protection while it struggled with ways to survive.

Seven months later, on May 19, 2005, it announced that it had agreed to merge with post- deregulation startup America West, with the combined airline to be based in Tempe, Arizona (America West's home city) but retaining the US Airways name. On September 16, 2005 a U.S. Bankruptcy Court Judge approved US Airways re-organization plan, effectively ending its bankruptcy filing and allowing the planned merger to take place on September 27, 2005.

The re-born US Airways did very well. By the end of September, 2006 it had an operating profit of $483 million, quite different from the previous quarter's $25 million loss. Which emboldened the new C.E.O., America West's W. Douglas Parker, to shock the entire industry by bidding $8 billion, later sweetened to $10 billion, to acquire venerable Delta Airlines, then in bankruptcy. As *The New York Times* reported, the deal would have made US Airways the largest airline in the world and allowed it to totally dominate East Coast air travel, as well as provide access to dozens of international destinations.

But the offer required approval not from shareholders but from Delta's creditors, who listened to the Delta CEO's pleas to "Let Delta Remain Delta." They voted against the offer, and on January 31, 2007 US Airways formally withdrew its bid. Then, in the second quarter of 2008, with oil at $120 per barrel, United and US Airways were once again floating the idea of a merger, although nothing substantive had occurred by the time this book went to press.

Anyone with even a passing interest in commercial aviation knows that today's airline industry is a totally different world from that which existed when the Locals existed. But what has happened to the concept of service to small communities? That is the topic of our final chapter.

Chapter 11: Ground Stopped

*B*y the end of 1989 the Local Service Airlines were gone. Oh, sure, US Air (it would not become US Airways until February 27, 1997) could trace its history back to Allegheny. But it no longer looked like nor felt like that feisty little local, and, to grab market share, its marketing people were more interested in how modern it was rather than in its history.

Not only were the locals gone, but so was the C.A.B. It had formally disappeared as of January 1, 1985, as stipulated in the Airline Deregulation Act of 1978. Actually, thanks to that law, it had lost oversight over route-granting three years earlier, on January 1, 1982, and authority over economic matters the year following, on January 1, 1983. Although the Departments of Transportation and of Justice have assumed some of the functions of the C.A.B., there is no longer any real control over routes and economic practices — except perhaps when mergers are involved. But deregulation meant just that — the removal of any regulation and the encouragement of a free market-based environment.

Which some saw as good and others as bad. Whatever! It is NOT the purpose of this chapter to re-hash the pros and cons of deregulation. *Rather this chapter will focus on the* quality *of scheduled airline service to the sort of communities once served by the Locals. Unfortunately, that 'quality' may grow even worse thanks to 2008's astronomical rise in fuel prices.*

The problems began decades before the 2008 fuel-price crisis. Although many of these communities were served by affiliates of the bigger airlines, such service was usually by a 'regional partner' of the major airline, and all too often these affiliates appeared on lists of 'worst-performance/most-delayed/most complained about.' The lack of service was exacerbated by insane fuel prices (at this writing crude oil was in excess of $130 per barrel, and jet fuel even higher) forcing more airlines to drastically seek ways to remain viable. In fact, as noted in our Introduction, the major airlines had announced that, after the summer travel season of 2008, they would be parking significant numbers of airplanes, and that led to warnings that the smaller communities would be seeing even more loss of service.

To be honest, many of the smaller communities are within driving distance of larger communities served by Low-Cost Carriers like AirTran, jetBlue, Southwest, etc., but reaching them requires a drive of one to two hours, unheard of in the era of the Local, when even small towns invested in airport improvements to keep convenient scheduled airline service.

So today, more than 50 years since the Locals received permanent certification, the U.S. airline industry is a totally different sort of creature. With this in mind, let's briefly examine the sad history of the declines in service to the sort of places that the Locals once proudly served.

Call it lawmaker's remorse. Some six months after deregulation took effect, some of those responsible were beginning to have doubts. Chief among these was the often-outspoken Senator Richard C. Byrd (D., West Virginia), then Senate Majority Leader, who told a Senate hearing that he regretted having voted for deregulation now that airlines were abandoning small communities. His colleague, Senator John Stennis (D., Mississippi), another former deregulation proponent, told *The New York Times,* "I think we made a great mistake here."

Oddly enough, the doomed C.A.B. disagreed. In its report issued a month earlier it claimed that service to all communities had increased "significantly." But the *Times* deflated that assertion. Although departures from small communities had increased, said the *Times*, they had increased only by 5.2%, significantly less than the industry-wide average of 8.4%. And many of those new departures were by commuter aircraft operating trips only to hub airports rather than flying short hops 'down-the-line' as the locals had done since their creation (see below). Also, the article asserted, 260 cities had lost some service in the year covered by the C.A.B. study.

It was a trend that would worsen. Years later author Paul S. Dempsey would note in *Flying Blind,* his analysis of deregulation, that "Transportation deregulation has meant isolation for many of America's rural communities. With the elimination of entry and exit regulation, airlines have been free to reduce their level of service to less lucrative communities and focus their energies and equipment on more profitable market opportunities." Communities that did not lose service nevertheless saw a marked change. Dempsey noted, "In many small towns, the larger airlines have disappeared, to be replaced by smaller commuter carriers, offering inferior levels of comfort, convenience, and safety. Small towns have seen a reduction in flights to all but medium and large hub cities."

By Department of Transportation definition, a "hub" can be any city with at least one-percent of all enplanements – and thus there are now 'small,' 'medium,' and 'large' hubs – everything else is a 'non-hub.' Non-hubs, of course, are many of the same places for which the C.A.B., four decades earlier, had created the local service concept. Now their government-mandated protection was gone and they were subject to the whims of the various airline accounting departments. As a result, Dempsey noted, "Between 1977 and 1984 flights between small hubs declined 2.9 percent, flights between small and non-hub cities fell 16.9 percent, and flights between non-hub cities dropped 6.9 percent."

To better understand "flights between non-hub cities" look at the 1950 route map of Mohawk's predecessor, Robinson. It offered travel around New York State before the Interstate was common. For example, from the state capital of Albany you could have flown Mohawk west to Utica or on to Syracuse, and from Syracuse down to Ithaca or to Corning – all without changing airplanes. The same trip would be impossible today. You <u>could</u> fly American Airlines from Albany to Chicago, and from there back east, but you'd land <u>not</u> in Syracuse but in Rochester, some 75 miles west. And the shortest such trip would take almost five-and-one-half hours, the same time required to fly New York City to Los Angeles.

This was certainly not the way it was supposed to be. The people who wanted deregulation did not want to see service to small communities disappear, and to prevent that they did create something called Essential Air Service (EAS). The concept was that any city receiving scheduled service from a certificated airline at the time deregulation went into effect would remain eligible for such service, leaving it up to the C.A.B. and later the Transportation Department to work out the details, including evaluating and selecting EAS candidates and determining the amount of subsidy as well as determining which cities get to keep their somewhat limited service.

But, under EAS rules, 'service' means an average of three round-trips per day aboard an aircraft of at least 19 seats to a major hub airport." Very often those 19-seat aircraft were Beechcraft 1900Ds. The Beech 1900D, lacking amenities like a lavatory and adequate headroom for six footers, makes even the DC-3 seem elegant. And, as noted above, these skinny flying tubes increasingly no longer operate intra-state flights. "No Convenient Route to Buffalo: Cancellation of Direct Flights From Albany Likely to Increase Time, Cost" read the June 21, 2007 headline of *The Albany Times-Union,* in upstate New York. Albany, the state capital, is 258 miles east of Buffalo, a major industrial center. The route, flown by Commutair operating as Continental Connection, was the only non-stop service between the two cities and had been used by 600 to 800 state employees per month. But Commutair was replacing its 19-seaters with larger aircraft, which it wanted to operate on longer and more profitable routes out of Cleveland.

Which fits in with deregulation's market-based philosophy. EAS rules allow airlines a fair amount of leeway to abandon routes, even though they are subsidized. Those subsidies are capped at a maximum of $200 per one-way passenger, unless a particular town is more than 210 miles from a large or medium hub. But rising fuel costs can outpace subsidies, especially if a particular city cannot generate enough use. In 2007 the town of Lancaster, not far from Philadelphia, was generating just 19 passengers for two daily departures, earning a per-passenger subsidy of just $136. "It supports air service nobody uses anyway," said industry analyst Mike Boyd, a vocal critic of EAS and other programs (see below).

But elected officials like to remain in office, and voting to end EAS could be a career-ending move. Yet it is often a victim of Washington budget games. Originally Congress allocated it an annual budget of $100 million for subsidies, but that amount had been whittled down to a $25 million annual budget until Congress doubled it in 1998. However, that $50 million had to <u>also</u> subsidize service to 26 communities in Alaska, cutting into the amount available to mainland communities. As a result, the per-passenger EAS is often inadequate. For example, the upstate New York city of Plattsburgh, not far from the resort area of Lake George, gets its only airline service from Cape Air, which offers three daily flights to Boston, Massachusetts on nine-seater Cessna turboprops. But while Cape Air says the trip costs approximately $94 per passenger, its EAS subsidy is only $73 per passenger. With the spiraling cost of fuel, that would be motivation for Cape Air to abandon Plattsburgh, as two EAS carriers had done before Cape Air arrived on the scene.

The reason that Plattsburgh qualifies for EAS subsidy is that it is 204 miles from Boston and 141 Miles from Albany, NY. Current EAS rules specify that a community must be a minimum of 70 miles from a large or medium hub airport to be eligible. But how to measure miles becomes a sticking point, as there are often several possible routes. Case in point: In 2007, Hagerstown, the very place that gave birth in 1967 to what would eventually become Allegheny Commuter (see Chapter 9: "A Slight Course Deviation") was in danger of losing its EAS status as it was deemed to be too close to a major airport. Various government-sponsored calculations put it at either 57 miles or 64 miles from Dulles International, too close by as little as six miles. But the State of Maryland claimed that, using the route that most people would drive, Hagerstown was actually 78 miles from Dulles. With the help of Maryland's representatives in Congress, the state's argument prevailed, and Hagerstown was deemed eligible to keep its $50 per passenger subsidy – until September 30, 2007. Eight months later Hagerstown had zero scheduled airline service, even though it had just renovated and extended its runway to 7,000 feet, hoping to attract regional jet service. In fact Hagerstown was the prime example in a *New York Times story citing cutbacks in service to small communities.*

On the flip side, however, critics note that Hagerstown boarded an average of just 16 passengers per day on its two daily departures, which is five times as many daily departing passengers as seen by Brookings, South Dakota. The Transportation Department and the State of South Dakota argued whether Brookings was 206 or 210 miles from Minneapolis-St. Paul International. At stake was a whopping $677 subsidy for the passengers who depart daily – all <u>three</u> of them. That amount prompted newly-elected Senator John Thune, a fiscally-conservative Republican, to argue that the taxpayer-funded largess should be re-instated. That's a "total waste of money," said Mike Boyd, pointing out that Brookings is just 57 miles from Sioux Falls Regional Airport. However, that field is technically not a hub, and thus cannot count, even though it's just an easy hour's drive on Interstate 29.

An hour's drive, and sometimes a drive of two or more hours, is part of the phenomenon called " Leakage" – a strange name for the obvious — that , with so many low-cost carriers, people will drive further to catch a lower fare. For example, Mesa Airlines canceled service to Gallup, New Mexico (pop. 20,000), just 122 miles northwest of Albuquerque and to Las Cruces (pop. 74,000), some 192 miles south. But Interstate 40 provides a high-speed route from Gallup to Albuquerque, just as Interstate 25 does from Las Cruces. People from both towns, accustomed to the distances of the American West, now drive to Albuquerque International, which is served by 12 carriers, including low fare Southwest – and Mesa.

Or take the example of the very upscale city of Naples, on the Gulf of Mexico in southwest Florida. When US Airways Express dropped its three daily Naples – Tampa flights in June 2003 it gave Naples an unfortunate claim to fame – the first city in Florida to lose all major airline service. But there is more here than meets the eye, for 'Neapolitans' can still travel by scheduled airline. All they have to do is make the drive to Fort Myers, some 30 miles north, where they will find Southwest Florida International Airport (RSW). In late 2007 that 20-year-old airport was served by 11 airlines – both low-cost <u>and</u> legacy carriers, plus weekly service by Germany's LTU. As old Hamlet said, "Ay, there's the rub." Does Naples deserve to plead hardship because the airlines have rejected it, or is it simply ignoring the new economic realities – airlines desperate to reduce costs will not duplicate service by serving airports 30 miles apart.

The Leakage phenomenon is not new; in fact it was the subject several years ago of a Government Accountability Office (GAO) study of air service at 202 smaller communities. That study reported that, east of the Mississippi River, over 70 percent of such communities were within a 100-mile drive to a hub or other large airport. West of the Mississippi that number fell dramatically to just 26 percent – but still 94 of the 202 communities studied nationwide were within the 100-mile radius of a larger airport.

The GAO researchers had solid empirical evidence from managers of the smaller airports. More than half said that leakage occurred to a great or even very-great extent and four-fifths felt that the possibility of lower fares was responsible. This being a government-sponsored study, its authors were not above citing the obvious – that there was more leakage at communities close to larger airports than at communities further away from such airports! The GAO study also noted, not surprisingly, that price-sensitivity overrides loyalty to place almost every time – at least for the infrequent-flying leisure traveler with two or three kids off to visit Grandma on Spring break.

But not for the 'road warriors' – frequently-traveling business people who need easy access to air travel. Someone with a 6:30 a.m. flight who first must drive an hour or more to the larger airport and must be there, as most airlines advise, at least 90 minutes before flight time, will have to set the alarm for 3:30 a.m. – not a happy thought. And what about area businesses encouraging out-of-town clients to visit? Telling a potential customer "We're just 90 minutes from the airport" will not create a very favorable impression. Any self-respecting local government and Chamber of Commerce would fight to bring scheduled airline service to the local airport. Which explains SCASDP.

In 1998, twenty years after the start of deregulation, a group of U.S. Senators – all Democrats – proposed the Air Service Restoration Act of 1998, to make improved air service to smaller communities a higher priority." The legislation proposed an Office of Small Community Air Service Development (hence SCASDP) to reverse the negative impact of deregulation on small town air service.

But it wasn't until April, 2000 that SCASDP became a reality, part of the AIR-21 Act signed into law during the Clinton administration. Funded with just $20 million initially, SCASDP rewards local initiative by providing grants to attract air service. To receive a grant, a community must demonstrate that it has already taken significant steps such as promoting local air service to the community and offering various types of financial incentives to attract air service. The incentives are supposed to provide revenue guarantees or operating cost offsets. In other words, a SCASDP grant enables a community to do on a purely local level what the C.A.B., with its operating subsidies, once did on a national level.

But there are some major differences between SCASDP and the 1944 C.A.B. decision that created the locals. SCASDP has a much smaller scope. Although a total of 147 communities applied in its first year, by law only 40 applicants could be selected, with no more than four from any one state. Then there are the philosophical differences. Where the C.A.B., operating on a New Deal model, dispensed federal largess, SCASDP is based more on a fiscally-conservative model. Washington will still dispense money, but in limited amounts, on a one-time-only non-renewable basis, and only to those communities which have demonstrated good-faith efforts to 'boot-strap,' i.e. to self-reliantly begin to solve a problem without outside assistance. SCASDP requires communities to submit detailed applications, even PowerPoint presentations, in order to be considered.

In its first year the highest SCASDP award was $1.5+ million grant to assist Bismarck, North Dakota in its efforts to promote regional service linking three contiguous Western states – North Dakota, South Dakota, and Montana. That, of course, was exactly what Frontier did in the 1950s, 60s, 70s, and 80s. The smallest award, $85 thousand, went to Abilene, Texas to hire a business development director to promote services at the local airport.

But all too often such efforts don't pay off. Take the example of Cumberland, Maryland (pop. 22,000), some 140 miles from Baltimore. In 2001 Cumberland lost all airline service, and local officials decided to act. They offered Boston-Maine Airways, operating as the Pan Am Connection, a bi-weekly payment of $170,268 if the airline would provide service to Baltimore-Washington International

(BWI) with three flights each weekday and two on Saturday/Sunday using 19seat British Aerospace Jetstream turboprops. It was a stupendous flop – with boardings dropping by half over six months. Modern Interstates bring BWI some two hours away, and so residents, including the local airport manager, opted to drive and save the cost of the additional airfare.

Which makes perfect sense to a more-practical, less-romantic industry observer like Mike Boyd, whose Boyd Group's "Regional Air Service: Adjusting to the New Realities" addresses the question of service to smaller communities. "Without question," that study says, "many US airports will irrevocably lose scheduled air service in the next decade....It is an economic fact that is in many cases driven by local consumers as well as by the airline industry." But, according to the Boyd analysis, this is not as dire a predicament as some indicate. The study differentiates between "local air service" and "access to the air transport system." Boyd's contention is that although airports may lose airline service, the community will still have access to the national air transport system via nearby hubs or regional airports, as in the case of Naples, Florida above.

Which, argues Boyd, makes programs like SCASDP unnecessary, especially when it provides funding for a community to initiate air service. That is exactly what two eastern Wyoming cities, Casper (pop. 49,600) and Gillette (pop. 19,600), did after receiving a half-million dollar SCASDP grant. They purchased a $1 million 19-seat Swearingen Metroliner which they then leased, at one-dollar-per-year, to Big Sky Airlines for trips to Billings, whose almost 90,000 population makes it Montana's largest city. The venture lasted 10 months, with Big Sky losing $50,000 per month. "The revenue just wasn't there," Big Sky's manager told the newspaper USA Today. Small wonder, as both cities are less than a half-day's interstate drive from Billings, with Casper some 230 miles away and Gillette some 180 miles.

The 1950's, 60's, and 70's are gone, Boyd argues, and the frequency and quality of service these communities once had from the locals just isn't coming back considering the costs involved in providing it. There are two sides to the issue, and it's easy to understand both. One wants to believe, as the C.A.B. did from 1944 on, that smaller communities deserve to have their own adequate air transportation. But one must also acknowledge that (1) for airlines suffering unprecedented economic losses providing such service is less and less feasible, and (2) that the continuing draw of the low cost carriers has changed the playbook, with passengers less concerned about convenience than fare. Those are the realities of a much-changed America some six decades after the C.A.B. first gave the go-ahead to the locals.

But what to say when confronted with stories like that of Ottumwa, Iowa. About 330 miles west of Chicago, Ottumwa (pop. 25,000) is a trade center for its region. But, tucked away in the southeast corner of the state, it is far from either of Iowa's two major Interstate highways. Two years ago the city lost its Essential Air Service subsidy because of excessive costs and, as a result, United Express pulled out of Ottumwa. But wait! Ottumwans still have access to airline service, if they first drive to Burlington-Southeast Iowa Regional (BRL), an hour away. The least onerous option available gives them the chance to board a 19seat Beech 1900-D United Express flight to Kansas City International (MCI), where, after a three-hour layover, they will then take a United Express regional jet from MCI to Chicago-O'Hare (ORD). A trip begun from BRL at noon will put that traveler into ORD at 5:00 p.m., provided there are no delays. Thus it would require almost an entire day (counting driving time and time to pass through security) to travel some 330 miles! Perhaps a price-sensitive once-per-year leisure traveler might chance it, but what does it mean for the frequently traveling business person?.

One Ottumwa manufacturer of construction equipment said that although the EAS-supported twice daily flights to Chicago were not always dependable, they did make it easier to do business. "When a customer asked how to get to Ottumwa we would reply ' United flies right in here.'," he told *The New York Times*. Now, he says, he sometimes has to charter an airplane to bring in customers, and he has relocated his sales force to cut travel expenses. Which further demonstrates that air travel is more than getting home for the holidays or taking the family on vacation. It is often an essential for conducting business, even if you're not a Fortune 500 company. In 1976, with deregulation fast approaching, *Flight*'s George Haddaway wrote:

"You can bet your bottom dollar that small-town America isn't going to stand by and watch air transport (under deregulation) …

abandon the functions so admirably performed by the local service airline industry for the towns of small and medium population." Obviously the late Mr. Haddaway, so often correct in his assessments, badly misjudged future developments.

Texarkana Regional Aiport (TXK), serving the twin cities of Texarkana, Arkansas and Texarakana, Texas, has a modicum of airline access. American Eagle operates four daily roundtrips to Dallas/Ft. Worth International (DFW) and Continental Connection operates two to Houston's George Bush International (IAH). But back in the heyday of the locals, Texarkana residents could fly Central not to some hub airport but to many communities in Texas and Oklahoma. Recently the TXK manager was hoping to get grant money to repair the 1936 terminal building. His plans were to have the old terminal become a museum, complete with a 1936 ticket counter, baggage carts, and flight schedules.

Perhaps that's a solution to declining small-community air service. Just as many small towns have made their now-unused railroad stations into restaurants, perhaps the growing number of towns who are losing all service could make their terminals into museums. They could hang up some memorabilia from one or more of the local service airlines so that residents can bring their children and say "See, we were once important enough to have our own airline service." It might help the younger generation connect to a long-gone era – an era when a government agency helped to create and nurture Airlines For the Rest of Us.

Bibliography

This book began life as an attempt at scholarly work, with endnotes for each chapter citing the research done. However, cooler heads prevailed, and as it underwent revision the decision was made to eliminate those endnotes – but to retain this bibliography. Hopefully the book will make the reader eager to read more about the Local Service Airlines, about the role of the C.A.B., about the effects of airline deregulation, about the aircraft that served the Locals so well, or about any other topic of the era. If so, the following lists offer a great place to start.

Books

> Bernstein, Aaron. Grounded: Frank Lorenzo and the Destruction of Eastern Airlines. New York, NY: Simon & Schuster, 1990.

> Burkhardt, Robert. The Civil Aeronautics Board. Dulles International Airport, VA: The Green Hills Publishing Company, Inc., 1974.

> Corbett, Donna. "Donald W. Nyrop: Airline Regulator, Airline Executive." Airline Executives and Federal Regulation. Ed. W. David Lewis. Columbus, OH: Ohio State U. Press, 2000.

> Davies, R.E.G. Continental Airlines: The First Fifty Years 1934-1984. Texas: Pioneer Publications, 1984.

> Davies, R.E.G., and I.E. Quastler. Commuter Airlines of the United States. Washington, D.C.: Smithsonian Institution Press, 1995.

> Davies, R.E.G.. "The DC-3 Replacement." <u>Fallacies and Fantasies of Air Transport Hisitory</u>. Comp. R.E.G. Davies. McLean, VA: Paladwyr Press, 1994.

> Davies, R.E.G.. <u>Airlines of the United States Since 1914</u>. Washington, D.C.: Smithsonian Institution Press, 1972.

> Dempsey, Paul Stephen and Goetz, Andrew R. <u>Airline Deregulation: Laissez-Faire Mythology</u>. Westport, CT: Quorum Books, 1992.

> Dempsey, Paul Stephen. <u>Flying Blind: The Failure of Airline Deregulation</u>. Washington, D.C.: Economic Policy Institute, 1990.

> Eads, George C.. <u>The Local Service Airline Experiment</u>. Washington, D.C.: The Brookings Institution, 1972.

> Gradidge, J.M.. <u>The Convairliners Story</u>. Kent, U.K.: Air-Britain Ltd., 1997.

> Jordan, William A.. <u>Airline Regulation in America: Effects and Imperfections</u>. Baltimore, MD: Johns Hopkins Press, 1970.

> Killion, Gary L. <u>The Martinliners</u>. Sand Point, ID: Airways International, 1998.

> Leary, William M.. "Robert E. Peach and Mohawk Airlines: A Study in Entrepreneurship." <u>Airline Executives and Federal Regulation</u>. Ed. W. David Lewis. Columbus, OH: Ohio State U. Press, 2000.

> Meyer, John R., and Clinton V. Oster, Jr.. <u>Deregulation and the New Airline Entrpreneurs</u>. Cambridge, MA: The MIT Press, 1984.

> Peterson, Barbara Sturken, and James Glab. <u>Rapid Descent: Deregulation and the Shakeout in the Airlines</u>. New York, NY: Simon and Schuster, 1994.

> Petzinger, Thomas, Jr.. <u>Hard Landing</u>. New York, NY: Random House, 1995.

> Robert E. Peach, "Four-Seaters to Fan Jets" Address to the Newcomen Society, New York, NY: The Newcomen Society, 1964

> Serling, Robert J.. <u>Ceiling Unlimited: The Story of North Central Airlines</u>. Walsworth Publishing, 1973

> Sharpe, M., and R. Shaw. <u>Boeing 737-100 and 200</u>. Osceola, WI: MBI Publishing, 2001.

> Smith, Jr., Myron L.. <u>Passenger Airliners of the United States 19261991</u>. Missoula, MT: Pictorial Histories Publishing Company, 1991.

> Waddington, Terry. <u>McDonnell Douglas DC-9</u>. Miami, FL: World Transport Press, 1998.

Articles

> Doug Scroggins. "Bonanza Air lines: Route of the Gold Strikes" <u>Airliners</u> 66: 58-63.

> Erickson, Charles, and Jon Proctor. " Mohawk Airlines - Route of the Air Chiefs." <u>Airliners</u> March/April, 1998: 24-36.

> Hill, Ronald C. "The First Frontier." <u>Airliners</u> January 2002: 44-55.

> Hurley, Richard J. "The Passing of the Pacemaker." <u>Airliners</u> Fall, 1988: 35 45.

> Jay, Charles. "Nuggets in the Sky… Local Service." <u>The Airline Pilot</u> June, 1954: 4-7.

> Elott, John. "Paul Bunyan's Airline: A Personal History." <u>Airways</u> July 1997: 53-60.

> Lanier, Alton. " Southern Airways: Route of the Aristocrats." <u>Airliners</u> March 1994: 26-34.

> Lusk, Brian. "Flying the Range." <u>Airliners</u> Spring, 1990: 35-40.

> Mellberg, Bill. " Herman's Story: A Short History of North Central Airlines." <u>Airliners</u> Fall 1992: 25-35.

> Mellberg, Bill. "Three Swallows Would Get You There: The Story of Ozark Airlines." <u>Airliners</u> Summer, 1990: > Minton, David H.. "This Little Piggy Went to the Bank." <u>Airliners</u> Fall, 1988: 26-35.

> Nichols, Dave. "Trans Texas Airways," <u>Airliners</u> July/August 2002: 42-49.

> Peck, Rand K. "Air New England: A Personal History." <u>Airways</u> November 1998L: 55-61.

> Proctor, Jon. "Air-West - A Tri-Merger." <u>Airliners</u> Jan./Feb. 2003: 36-47.

> Proctor, Jon. "Air West 'Top Banana' - pt. II." <u>Airliners</u> March 2003: 26-37.

> Solomon, Stan. "A Local for Every Locale." <u>Airways</u> October, 2000:

> Solomon, Stan. " Frontier Airlines – Made the West Less Wild." Airways February 2002: 49-56.

> Stevens, William K.. No Longer Tree-Top Airways." The New York Times 08 November 1978, natl. ed.: D1.

> Turner, Walter R.. "A Brief History of Piedmont Airlines." Carolina Comments September, 2001: 104-111. Government Publications

> United States. Bureau of Regulatory Operations .Airline Pricing Under Board Fare Policies: Part I. History of Board Fare Policy. Washington, D.C.: Civil Aeronautics Board, 1978.

> United States. CAB Reports, Vol. 20. Continental – Pioneer Acquisition Case Docket No. 6457 et. al.. Washington, D.C.: USGPO, 1959.

> United States. CAB Reports, Vol. 47. Frontier – Central Merger, Docket 18517. Washington, D.C.: USGPO, 1967.

> United States. CAB Reports, Vol. 48. Allegheny – Lake Central Merger Case, Docket 19151. Washington, D.C.: USGPO, 1968.

> United States. CAB Reports, Vol. 48. Bonanza – Pacific – West Coast Merger Case, Docket 18996. Washington, D.C.: USGPO, 1968.

> United States. CAB Reports, Vol. 59. Allegheny – Mohawk Merger Case, Dockets 23682. 23371. Washington, D.C.: USGPO, 1972.

> United States. Commercial Aviation: Factors Affecting Efforts to Improve Air Service at Small Community Airports, GAO-03-330. Washington, D.C.: Government Accounting Office, 2003.

> United States. Permanent Certificates for Local Service Air Carriers," Hearings before a Subcommittee of the Committee on Interstate and Foreign Commerce on S.R. 651, The U.S. Senate, 84th Congress, 1st Session, Feb. 21 and 24, 1955. Washington, D.C.: USGPO, 1955.

> Wynns, Peyton L. . United States. Office of Transportation Regulatory Policy. Air Service to Small Communities. Washington, D.C.: , U.S. D. o. T., 1976.

Appendix 1 : Museum Pieces

Despite the hundred-plus aviation museums found throughout this country, it is not as easy to find preserved airliners as it is preserved military and general aviation aircraft. Of course there are notable exceptions, such as the wonderful collections at the National Air & Space Museum's Dulles Extension and Seattle's Museum of Flight. Otherwise, perhaps for economic reasons or just because of their relatively large size, commercial aircraft are not readily found in aviation museums. And finding them is a matter of luck, as, to this author's best knowledge, there are no published guides.

Which makes this Appendix valuable for fans of Local Service equipment. Of the hundreds of airplanes that flew for the locals, a handful have been saved as museum pieces…and one as a restaurant attraction. Some have been restored in the colors of a local or regional. Others flew for a Local but now bear the markings of a legacy carrier – hence the "ex-" prefix in the title.

NB: Although the information below is as complete and up-to-date as possible, it is always a good idea to verify with that particular museum whether that airplane is still part of its collection.

<u>A Piedmont DC-3</u> – The Carolinas Aviation Museum (CAM), at North Carolina's Charlotte-Douglas International, features the beautifully restored Piedmont DC-3 which graced the cover of *Airways*' magazine October, 2000 issue. Although the airplane never

flew for Piedmont, that airline purchased it from Besler Aviation in 1987 for restoration in their 50's-era livery with tail number N44V. On December 17, 1997 (the 94th anniversary of the Wright Brothers flight) CAM, which had bought the airplane from USAir in 1996, used it to transport Piedmont's Tom Davis to Kitty Hawk for ceremonies inaugurating him into the National Aviation Hall of Fame. And a year later, on February 20, 1998, N44V again flew Davis, this time from Wilmington to Charlotte, to mark the 50th anniversary of Piedmont's inaugural flight. The airplane was born as a C-47 (41-38596) and delivered to the Army Air Force on July 22, 1942. It was 'discharged' two years later and spent the next 43 years, until Piedmont's acquisition, operating for a series of private owners.

An Ozark DC-3 – The Prairie Aviation Museum (PAM), in Bloomington, Illinois, features N763A, a DC-3 in Ozark's classic green-and-white. But this particular airplane actually never flew for Ozark. It began life on March 11, 1942 as a Navy C-53 (MSN 4894) but was transferred to the Navy as an R4D-3. It served at various Naval Air Stations on the east coast. Four years later it was sold by the War Assets Administration to Continental, which registered it NC73726. On August 31, 1949 Continental sold it to Southern, which would operate it for the next 17 years, re-registering it N70SA on May 14, 1957. Southern sold it on August 25, 1966 and it traded hands several times before being acquired by PAM in February 1984. Museum volunteers flew it to Bloomington, where they spent a year plus cleaning it up. Then, on September 16, 1985 Ozark asked to borrow it to help celebrate their 35th anniversary. As part of the arrangement Ozark repainted it in 50s-era Ozark colors and registered it N763A. Three months later, it was returned to PAM, where it remains today as the museum's "ambassador" offering flights. It is listed on the National Park Service's National Register of Historic Places and has the distinction of being the only flyable aircraft on that register.

A Pacific Martin 404 – Another flyable example in authentic local colors, N636X began life as MSN 14135, delivered to TWA on July 16, 1952 and registered N40429. Dubbed *Skyliner Peoria,* she served with TWA until March 10, 1959. A Dayton, Ohio company purchased it, registered it N636, and converted it to a luxury 16-seat executive transport whose extra-range tanks enabled it to become the first Martin 404 to cross the Atlantic Ocean. A later owner, the father of the current owner, operated it as a luxury charter aircraft. It was eventually stored at Pueblo, Colorado where the current owner, Jeff Whitesell purchased it in June, 1994. Whitesell, a Delta pilot, started Airliners of America, which restored the Martin, now registered N636X, in Pacific Air Lines markings. Based for many years at Camarillo Airport, between Los Angeles and Santa Barbara, the airplane was recently flown to the Planes of Fame Air Museum at Arizona's Grand Canyon/Valle Airport.

A Piedmont 737 – Indoors and forever protected from the elements is just part of an ex-Piedmont Boeing 737-200. Serial number 20213 was delivered April 29, 1969 to Piedmont and registered N744N. After US Air acquired Piedmont the airplane was re-registered N213US. In July, 1995 US Air donated the airplane to Seattle's Museum of Flight. Five years later the Museum formally dedicated its "737 Airliner Theater" – the fuselage from nose to wing-root. Fitted with first class seats in a 2 x 2 configuration, the fuselage provides a comfortable place for visitors to relax and watch some fascinating documentaries about commercial aviation.

An ex- Southern Martin 404 – The Airline History Museum at Kansas City (AHM), which began life as the Save-A-Connie organization, now boasts, besides its gleaming Lockheed Constellation, a gleaming Martin 404 – both in the white-with-red-stripe livery reminiscent of TWA's. Although this particular Martin (14142) never flew for TWA it did fly for Eastern and for Southern, which is why it is included here. Delivered to Eastern on January 31, 1953 (N451A) it served there for nine years before being sold to Southern on September 5, 1961, registered N145SA. It spent 16 years with Southern before being sold on May 25, 1978. Save A Connie acquired it on September 17, 1990, lovingly restored it, and now AHM operates it as "Skyliner Kansas City."

An ex- North Central DC-3 – Kansas City's Airline History Museum (above) has acquired a former TWA DC-3 and is restoring it to its former glory. The airplane, msn 3294, was built in February, 1941 and delivered to TWA on March 4, 1941, registered NC 1945. It flew for TWA as ship 386 until 1952, when it was acquired by North Central. After a 14-year career with North Central it was sold to a charter operator and then to travel club Coronado Airlines. Eventually it was put out to pasture at Roswell, New Mexico where AHM members discovered it, purchased it, and had it trucked to Kansas City. The airplane needs extensive renovation but AHM member-volunteers hoped to have it join the Connie and the Martin in 2005.

An ex- Mohawk Convair 240 – Many visitors to California's Castle Air Museum (in Atwater, two hours from San Francisco) admire the Convair HC-131A, the U.S. Coast Guard's version of the C-131A, gleaming in white and red. Some may know that this handsome specimen once was Mohawk's "Air Chief Pequot," a Convair 240-11, N1018C, msn. 133. It was acquired by Mohawk on October 18, 1956 from Swissair, which had taken delivery of it on February 17, 1949. Mohawk sold it to Fairchild-Hiller on December 31, 1966, and it eventually flew for a travel club in Modesto, California. Then in 1979 it landed in a cornfield, some 3.7 miles short of Modesto's runway, where it remained for 19 years as one effort after another to 'rescue' it failed economically. Finally in 2000 the property owner donated it to Castle Air Museum, which decided to honor the U.S. Coast Guard by restoring it as CG 5785.

An ex- Southern Martin 404 – Another former Southern airplane graces the airfield at Reading, Pennsylvania, where volunteers of the Mid Atlantic Air Museum (MAAM) have restored the airplane in the colors of Eastern Air Lines. This particular ship, #14141, was delivered to Eastern on January 23, 1952. Eastern registered it N450A and flew it for almost ten years before selling it to Southern on December 20, 1962. Ironically, Southern put it into service as of January 21, 1963 – almost eleven years to the date it was first delivered to Eastern. Southern registered it N149S and flew it nine more years until putting it in storage at Atlanta. MAAM acquired it in 1991, repainted it in that spectacular 50's-era Eastern livery, and flies it around the air show circuit.

An Allegheny Convair 580 – Also at Reading, Pennsylvania's Mid Atlantic Air Museum is a Convair 580 which the museum intended to repaint in Allegheny colors once funding became available. This particular airplane, msn. 202, was built July 15, 1954 as a Cv340B/440, but never saw airline service. Instead it joined the corporate world, spending its first nine-plus years with a series of private owners. Converted as a 580 in February, 1963 it eventually became the personal airplane of Malcolm Forbes, publisher of Forbes Magazine. Painted gold and black, it also bore the magazine's famed "Capitalist Tool" slogan plus a registration of N60FM. The Forbes organization operated it from 1970 to 974, when it was purchased by McDonnell Douglas Corporation. It eventually spent many years as an aerial mapping and survey aircraft for the U.S. Department of Energy.

An ex- Trans-Texas DC-3 – To commemorate the 2003 Centennial of Flight, Continental donated its award-winning (Grand Champion Antique, Oshkosh 1997) DC-3A to the Lone Star Flight Museum of Galveston, Texas. Although it wears Continental colors, the airplane is former Trans-Texas, N25673, msn. 2213. TTA purchased the ship on November 11, 1947 from American, its first owner, which took delivery in May, 1940. She served 21+ years as a TTA " Starliner" before being sold to an aircraft broker in February, 1969. In 1974 Provincetown-Boston Airways acquired the airplane, re-registered her as N130PB, and flew her until November, 1988. Continental obtained the airplane in 1989, restored it, and flew it to airshows as a promotional piece. Continental's press release announcing their donation acknowledged Trans-Texas as a "predecessor" of Continental, which is sure to bring a wry grin to the lips of any aviation history buff (see Chapter 10, "Off the Radar Scope"). Legend has it that this was the same airplane on whose wing a bevy of TTA 'cowgirl' hostesses appeared in a 1950s Trans-Texas ad.

A Multi-Owner Martin 404 – Well, it's a better fate than the wrecker's ball. A Martin 404, #14164, which once served three locals, now spends its days, minus flying surfaces, indoors resting in a downtown San Francisco watering hole/restaurant called the Caribbean Zone. Built in April, 1952 it spent almost ten years with Eastern Airlines as N743A. It was sold to Mohawk on September 18, 1961, reregistered N467M, and placed in service a week later as *Air Chief Ottawa*. It was sold to Ozark three years later, on October 26, 1964 where it served for 2.5

years before being sold to Fairchild Hiller on March 11, 1967. Fairchild stored it at Las Vegas before leasing it to Piedmont on May 20, 1967. It served as Cherokee Pacemaker for a year before being returned to Fairchild. Eventually it was leased to The Doobie Brothers rock band before being withdrawn from use and dismantled in 1986.

An ex- North Central DC-3 – Old 728 – On May 28, 1975 North Central officially retired "Old 728," a.k.a. N21728, a Douglas DC3 that was then the world's high-time aircraft with 84,875 hours of flying time in its logbook. It had worn out 550 tires, 25,000 spark plugs, and 136 engines. The aircraft had been in scheduled airline service since August of 1939. It already had logged 51,398 miles when North Central bought it, in March, 1952, from Eastern Airlines. Then North Central put another 31,634 miles on her in 13 years. True to form, the gallant old lady spent her final day hard at work. She operated three flight numbers, including North Central's early-morning (0625 hrs.) Flight 2 from Milwaukee to Chicago and finishing her day, flown by one of Wisconsin Central's original pilots, at Minneapolis some 16 hours later. But the airplane's working days weren't over. North Central made her into an 11-seat executive transport and put another 1843 miles on her before donating her to the Henry Ford Museum in Dearborn, Michigan in 1975, where she rests in a place of honor, although inaccurately wearing the markings of Northwest Airlines.

Appendix 2: Locals On the Web

As you might have known (or suspected), there are many Web sites dedicated to the Locals. Some are stand-alone sites, labors of love created by former employees to record for posterity the story of their former employer. There are also briefer entries about many of the Locals on Wikipedia.org, the digital encyclopedia. And deep within the US Airways website are some excellent histories of US Airways parent Allegheny and the Locals it absorbed as it continued to grow. Many of these sites will provide additional information, photos, memories, etc. and are definitely worth perusing.

Below, in alphabetical order, appear lists of, first, the stand-alone Web sites, then the Wikipedia.org pages, and finally the pages on the US Airways site.

NB: All listed sites were 'active' as this book was in preparation, June, 2008. *Airlines For the Rest Of Us* bears no responsibility for the disappearance and/or non-accessibility of any site listed. Finally, please type the URL carefully; unfortunately, it is not yet possible to click a link on a paper page!

Stand-Alone Sites

Arizona Airways
http://fal-1.tripod.com/ Arizona.html
Bonanza
http://www.bonanzaairlines.com/
Central
http://lamkins.tripod.com/CentralAirlines.html
http://lamkins.tripod.com/CNcollection.html

Challenger
http://jakeroo.tripod.com/ Challenger.html

Frontier
http://fal-1.tripod.com/

Mohawk
http://www.kamienski.net/mohawk/map.html

Monarch
http://jakeroo.tripod.com/ Monarch.html

North
Central http://www.hermantheduck.org/

Ozark
http://www.ozarkairlines.com/

Pacific
http://www.time.com/time/printout/0,8816,799355,00.html

Piedmont
http://www.jetpiedmont.com/
http://www.carolinasaviation.org/collections/aircraft/dc3n44v.html

Southern
http://www.southernairways.org/

Hughes AirWest
http://www.hughesairwest.com/

Republic
http://www.mnhs.org/library/findaids/00358.html

On Wikipedia.org

Allegheny
http://en.wikipedia.org/wiki/ Allegheny_Airlines

Bonanza
http://en.wikipedia.org/wiki/Bonanza_Air_Lines

Central
http://en.wikipedia.org/wiki/Central_Airlines

Lake Central
http://en.wikipedia.org/wiki/Lake_Central_Airlines

Mohawk
http://en.wikipedia.org/wiki/ Mohawk_Airlines

North Central
http://en.wikipedia.org/wiki/North_Central_Airlines

Ozark
http://en.wikipedia.org/wiki/ Ozark_Airlines

Pacific
http://en.wikipedia.org/wiki/ Pacific_Air_Lines
http://en.wikipedia.org/wiki/ Pacific_Air_Lines#External_links

Piedmont
http://en.wikipedia.org/wiki/Piedmont_Airlines_%281948-1989%29

Pioneer
http://en.wikipedia.org/wiki/ Pioneer_Airlines

Southern
http://en.wikipedia.org/wiki/ Southern_Airways

Texas International (Trans-Texas)
http://en.wikipedia.org/wiki/Texas_International_Airlines
West Coast
http://en.wikipedia.org/wiki/West_Coast_Airlines

Airwest / Hughes Airwest
http://en.wikipedia.org/wiki/ Hughes_Airwest

Republic
http://en.wikipedia.org/wiki/Republic_Airlines_%281979-1986%29

On US Airways site:

Allegheny
http://www.usairways.com/awa/content/aboutus/pressroom/history/ allegheny.aspx

Lake Central
http://www.usairways.com/awa/content/aboutus/pressroom/history/ lakecentral.aspx

Mohawk
http://www.usairways.com/awa/content/aboutus/pressroom/history/ mohawk.aspx

Piedmont
http://www.usairways.com/pv_obj_cache/pv_obj_id_1516B41E5B8B938A632C306238674FD9DD990000/filename/Piedmont_Airlines.pdf

Index

A

Airline Deregulation 56, 104, 123, 135
airmail 17, 30, 31, 91
Air Chief 36, 55, 80, 141, 142
Air New England 7, 23, 24, 56, 57, 100, 106, 112, 113, 136
air taxi 15, 24, 101
Air West 51, 56, 88, 100, 103, 107, 108, 136
Allegheny xi, 5, 16, 18, 32, 35, 40, 45, 47, 55, 56, 73, 74, 75, 76, 94, 95, 97, 99, 100, 101, 102, 103, 109, 110, 123, 127, 137, 141, 142, 144, 146, 147
Allegheny Commuter 56, 76, 101, 102, 127
All American 17, 29, 95
American x, xi, 3, 8, 10, 11, 16, 17, 29, 31, 32, 36, 41, 45, 49, 50, 73, 80, 86, 91, 95, 99, 109, 119, 125, 128, 133, 142
Arizona xiii, 8, 9, 25, 31, 56, 78, 103, 121, 140, 145

B

BAC One-Eleven 48, 49, 75, 80
Barnes 35, 102
Beech 19, 20, 21, 23, 24, 26, 74, 75, 101, 102, 103, 104, 126, 132
Bez 3, 10, 11, 41, 46, 51, 83, 88, 107, 108
Boeing 247D 25
Boeing 727 48, 51, 84, 108
Boeing 737 48, 51, 73, 135, 140
Bonanza Air Lines 22
Braniff 7, 23, 38, 50, 96, 101, 113
Buffalo 15, 16, 30, 31, 77, 126
Burr 113, 115, 116, 117
By-pass Authority 97

C

C.A.B. x, xi, 1, 2, 3, 4, 5, 6, 7, 8, 9, 10, 11, 12, 13, 14, 15, 16, 17, 18, 19, 20, 21, 22, 23, 24, 26, 29, 31, 32, 33, 36, 37, 38, 39, 40, 49, 50, 52, 54, 57, 88, 90, 91, 92, 93, 94, 95, 96, 97, 98, 99, 100, 101, 102, 106, 107, 108, 109, 110, 111, 113, 114, 118, 123, 124, 125, 126, 130, 131, 132, 134
central 15, 54, 95, 97
Challenger 8, 9, 25, 145
Civil Aeronautics Board x, 1, 134, 137
Clergy Fares 94
Combs 103
Continental x, 18, 31, 38, 39, 54, 86, 99, 101, 115, 116, 117, 126, 133, 134, 137, 139, 142

Convair 240 12, 20, 46, 141
Convair 340 28, 37, 46, 47, 106, 109
Convair 440 48
Convair 540 47
Convair 580 46, 73, 79, 103, 141
Convair 600 12, 20, 46, 73, 106
Converse 22, 77, 107

D

Davis 12, 13, 34, 41, 48, 55, 139
DC-3 replacement 47
DC-9 12, 48, 51, 52, 53, 56, 73, 76, 82, 85, 86, 87, 96, 113, 136
Delta x, xiii, 18, 24, 51, 52, 111, 121, 140
Department of Transportation 118, 119, 120, 121, 125
deregulation 92, 98, 101, 104, 111, 114, 116, 121, 123, 124, 125, 126, 129, 132, 134
Docket 857 4, 8, 11, 17
DuPont 16, 17, 99

E

EAS 126, 127, 132
Eastern 13, 18, 26, 33, 40, 42, 43, 46, 91, 97, 99, 111, 115, 119, 134, 140, 141, 142, 143
Empire 11, 25
Essair 7, 8, 17, 29
Essential Air Service xi, 90, 92, 126, 132
experiment x, 4, 7, 17, 29, 39, 93, 104, 116

F

Fairchild F-27 48, 51, 73
fares xii, 2, 28, 93, 94, 95, 111, 114, 116, 118, 129
feeder 7, 8, 14, 15, 16, 25, 74, 111, 115, 120
Feldman 101, 115, 116
Flag Stops 95
Flight magazine 5, 19, 29, 96, 101

Florida xiii, 18, 19, 26, 30, 82, 104, 128, 131
Four Wheel Drive Company 14
Friendship 23, 40, 55
Frontier 5, 7, 8, 9, 25, 30, 40, 46, 51, 52, 56, 73, 77, 78, 79, 94, 98, 100, 101, 103, 104, 105, 106, 107, 115, 116, 117, 130, 136, 137, 145

G

Gas Light Service 81
George Haddaway 28, 42, 96, 132
Go-Getter 52, 53, 119
Guaranteed Loan Act 33, 40

H

Hamilton 23
Hayward 9
helicopter 6, 33, 36, 55, 80, 109
Herman 53, 81, 136
Hughes 108, 111, 146, 147
Hughes Air West 108
Hulse 18, 19, 30, 86, 111

I

Icahn 118, 119
intrastate 7, 8, 14, 15, 22, 23, 25, 55, 120

K

K Kahle 19, 20

L

LaGuardia 50, 85
Lake Central 20, 21, 27, 29, 47, 55, 73, 76, 79, 80, 100, 109, 110, 120, 137, 146, 147
Leakage 128, 129
Lil Moh 80
Lorenzo 12, 56, 113, 114, 115, 116, 117, 119, 134

150

M

major x, xiii, 7, 38, 90, 96, 97, 104, 109, 113, 115, 120, 124, 126, 127, 128, 130, 132
Martin 2-0-2 37, 38, 39, 54
Martin 4-0-4 28, 48, 55
Medford 10, 11, 88, 107
merger 8, 9, 11, 21, 39, 56, 81, 83, 86, 107, 108, 109, 110, 111, 113, 118, 119, 120, 121, 122
Metropolitan 48
Mid-West 13, 25
Miniliners 103
Mohawk x, 15, 16, 26, 35, 36, 37, 40, 42, 43, 44, 45, 47, 48, 49, 50, 51, 55, 73, 74, 76, 80, 81, 94, 97, 100, 102, 103, 109, 110, 115, 120, 125, 135, 136, 137, 141, 142, 145, 146, 147
Monarch 7, 8, 9, 25, 145

N

New York Air 115
New York City xi, 15, 16, 25, 82, 84, 95, 97, 125
non-hub 125
Nonstop Authority 96
Nord 262A 47
Northeast x, 24, 26
North Central xii, 5, 13, 14, 15, 21, 25, 40, 45, 53, 81, 92, 94, 95, 100, 108, 110, 111, 135, 136, 140, 141, 143, 146

O

outgrow 37
Ozark 22, 23, 27, 32, 33, 41, 45, 46, 48, 52, 53, 55, 74, 81, 82, 83, 97, 100, 104, 117, 118, 119, 120, 136, 139, 142, 145, 146

P

Pacemaker x, 48, 84, 136, 143
Pacemaster 38, 54
Pacific 3, 9, 10, 11, 25, 33, 39, 41, 45, 46, 51, 54, 55, 56, 83, 88, 92, 94, 95, 100, 107, 108, 137, 139, 140, 145, 146
Pamper Jet 56
Peach 16, 35, 36, 48, 49, 50, 80, 110, 115, 135
Peanuts 95, 114
Penn Commuter 47
PEOPLExpress 113, 115, 116, 117
Permanent Certification 4, 24, 32, 37, 124
Pick-up 3, 16, 17
Pioneer 7, 8, 10, 24, 29, 30, 31, 33, 37, 38, 39, 54, 84, 95, 106, 134, 137, 147
pressurized 37, 40, 41, 42
promotional fares 93

R

Robinson 15, 16, 80, 125
R regional 131, 138

S

SCASDP 129, 130, 131
short haul 5
Small Community Air Service Development 129
Southern x, xii, 11, 18, 19, 26, 30, 31, 42, 55, 73, 81, 84, 85, 86, 97, 100, 108, 110, 111, 119, 136, 139, 140, 141, 145, 147
Southwest 9, 10, 11, 37, 39, 40, 54, 95, 121, 124, 128
Starliner 142
subsidized xi, 90, 91, 101, 126
subsidy 2, 15, 24, 26, 37, 38, 39, 40, 41, 50, 91, 92, 96, 97, 98, 99, 100, 102, 106, 109, 110, 112, 126, 127, 128, 132
suicide 110, 115, 116
Summit 9
Swallows 119, 136

Sweaty Palms 83

T

terminated 25, 26, 104
Texas Air Corporation 115, 117, 119
Texas International 12, 86, 95, 100, 104, 111, 113, 114, 115, 147
The Flying Interurban 29, 80
Trans-Texas 12, 42, 56, 74, 87, 91, 94, 95, 113, 142, 147
trunk 5, 8, 11, 13, 24, 29, 30, 32, 38, 42, 44, 48, 53, 93, 96, 97, 115
TTA 12, 91, 113, 142
Turbomeca 47, 76
turboprop 40, 41, 45, 46, 47, 48, 52, 55, 73
Turner 20, 21, 27, 137
two-minute stops 10

U

United x, xi, 1, 3, 10, 28, 38, 88, 91, 96, 100, 101, 111, 116, 117, 121, 132, 134, 135, 137
US Airways xi, 5, 16, 120, 121, 123, 128, 144, 147

V

Visit USA 93, 94

W

West Coast xii, 3, 10, 11, 25, 33, 40, 41, 43, 46, 51, 55, 56, 73, 74, 76, 83, 87, 88, 92, 100, 103, 107, 108, 137, 147
Whitney 24, 47, 76, 112
Wiggins 25, 26
Wine Cellar Service 53
Wisconsin Central 5, 13, 14, 92, 143
WWII 28, 87

Y

YS-11A 48, 55, 73

Z

Zimmerly 25

Made in the USA
Columbia, SC
18 March 2024